Bentham's Theory of the Modern State

HARVARD POLITICAL STUDIES

Published under the direction of the
Department of Government in Harvard University

ntham's Theory of the Modern State

NANCY L. ROSENBLUM

Harvard University Press

Cambridge, Massachusetts, and London, England

1978

Library of Congress Cataloging in Publication Data

Rosenblum, Nancy L 1947-
    Bentham's theory of the modern state.

    (Harvard political studies)
    Includes bibliographical references and index.
    1. Bentham, Jeremy, 1748-1832. 2. Law—Philos-
ophy. 3. Utilitarianism. 4. State, The. I. Title. II. Series.
K334.R68   320.1'092'4   77-17034
ISBN 0-674-06665-0

To Richard

Acknowledgments

Since my undergraduate days Judith Shklar has given me invaluable direction, encouragement, and counsel, and I am indebted to her above all. Harvey C. Mansfield, Jr., and Michael Walzer both gave me useful critical comments on an earlier version of this manuscript, for which I am grateful. And I owe special thanks to two friends: Stephen Schuker patiently tried to teach me the rudiments of style and urged me to attend to them; Arthur Jacobson listened often to my ideas on Bentham and generously shared his own with me. The assistance and goodwill of Aida DiPace Donald at Harvard University Press have made this publishing venture a pleasure.

I wish to thank the National Endowment for the Humanities for a summer grant in 1974. An earlier version of Chapter 2 appeared as "Bentham's Social Psychology for Legislators," in *Political Theory,* 1, No. 2 (May 1973), 171-185, and the publisher, Sage Publications, Inc., has given me permission to use parts of it here. The "Guide to the Bowring Edition" was compiled by David Lyons and appears in his book, *In the Interest of the Governed* (© Oxford University Press, 1973); it is reprinted by permission of the Oxford University Press.

Contents

Short Forms of Citation and
Guide to the Bowring Edition   xi

Introduction   1

1. A Utilitarian Code of Law: Ordinary or
   Extraordinary Legislation?   9

2. A Social Psychology for Legislators   27

3. Antilegal Ideologies   55

4. Sovereignty and Law   72

5. The Sovereign State   99

6. Responsible Public Service   118

Conclusion   151

Notes   157

Index   167

Short Forms of Citation and
Guide to the Bowring Edition

References to Bentham's writings appear in the text. Wherever possible I have cited *The Works of Jeremy Bentham,* published under the superintendence of his executor, John Bowring, 11 vols. (New York: Russell & Russell, 1962, reproduced from the Bowring edition of 1838-1843). *The Works* is the most commonly available source of Bentham's writings. For the sake of consistency, and for the reader's convenience, I have cited the Bowring *Works* even in the case of *An Introduction to the Principles of Morals and Legislation,* which has been revised by editors J. H. Burns and H. L. A. Hart (London: Athlone Press, 1970). A great deal has been written about the unreliability of the Bowring volumes and a complete and scholarly edition, *The Collected Works of Jeremy Bentham,* is being prepared under the direction of general editor J. H. Burns and published by Athlone Press. For the present, however, Bowring remains the major source for the full range of Bentham's writings, and it is not so inaccurate as to make Bentham's thought inaccessible. References to the Bowring edition appear by volume and page number.

The following works by Bentham are cited frequently by the short titles indicated:

Correspondence	*The Correspondence of Jeremy Bentham,* vol. I (1752-1776) and vol. II (1770-1780), ed. T. L. S. Sprigge (London: Athlone Press, 1968), and vol. III (1781-1788), ed. Ian Christie (London: Athlone Press, 1971)
Stark	*Jeremy Bentham's Economic Writings,* ed. W.

	Stark, 3 vols. (London: Allen & Unwin, 1952-1954)
OLG	*Of Laws in General,* ed. H. L. A. Hart (London: Athlone Press, 1970)
TL	*The Theory of Legislation,* ed. C. K. Ogden (New York: Harcourt, Brace, 1931)

Guide to the Bowring Edition

The guide to the Bowring edition was compiled by David Lyons and appears in his book, *In the Interest of the Governed* (Oxford University Press, 1973); it is reprinted here by permission of the Oxford University Press.

GUIDE TO THE BOWRING EDITION. No such guide seems otherwise available, even in the edition itself. It indicates most of Bentham's publications during his lifetime (dates are of the first appearance of previously published works, according to the best available information).

Volume I

General Preface, by W.W., v-xv.

List of Errata, 1-2.

Introduction to the Study of the Works of Jeremy Bentham, by John Hill Burton, 3-83.

An Introduction to the Principles of Morals and Legislation, 1789, i-xiii, 1-154. (Text from 1823 edn., with insertions from Dumont's *Traites;* see sect. I.B, below.)

Essay on the Promulgation of Laws, 155-68. (Based on MSS. and printed works.)

Essay on the Influence of Time and Place in Matters of Legislation, 169-94. (Based on MSS.)

A Table of the Springs of Action, 1817, 195-219.

A Fragment on Government 1776, 221-95. (Text from 1823 edn., with added Historical Preface.)

Principles of the Civil Code, 297-364. (Based on Dumont's *Traites* and MSS., with Appendix, Of the Levelling System.)

Principles of Penal Law, 365-580. (Based on Dumont's *Traites* and *Theorie* and MSS., here with Appendix, On Death-Punishment, published 1831.)

Volume II

Principles of Judicial Procedure, 1-188. (Based on MSS.)

The Rationale of Reward, 1825, 189-266. (Based on Dumont's *Theorie,* here with added Appendix.)

Leading Principles of a Constitutional Code, 1823, 267-74.

On the Liberty of the Press, and Public Instruction, 1821, 275-97.

An Essay on Political Tactics, 299-373. (Based on Dumont's *Tactique* and MSS., fragment published 1791.)

The Book of Fallacies, 1824, 375-487.

Anarchical Fallacies, 489-534. (Originally in Dumont's *Tactique.*)

Principles of International Law, 535-60. (Based on MSS., here with Appendix, Junctiana Proposal.)

A Protest Against Law-Taxes, 1795, 573-83.

Supply without Burden, 1795, 585-98.

Tax with Monopoly, 599-600.

Volume III

Defense of Usury, 1787, 1-29.

A Manual of Political Economy, 31-84. (Based on Dumont's *Theorie* and MSS.)

Observations on the Restrictive and Prohibitory Commercial System, 1821, 85-103.

A Plan . . . [Circulating Annuities, &c.], 105-53. (Based on MSS.)

A General View of a Complete Code of Laws, 155-210. (Based on MSS. and various printed works.)

Pannomial Fragments, 211-30. (Based on MSS.)

Nomography, 231-95. (Based on MSS., here with Appendix, Logical Arrangements.)

Equity Dispatch Court Proposal, 1830, 297-317.

Equity Dispatch Court Bill, 319-431. (Based on MSS.)

Plan of Parliamentary Reform, 1818, 433-557.

Radical Reform Bill, 1819, 558-97.

Radicalism not Dangerous, 599-622. (Based on MSS.)

Volume IV

A View of the Hard-Labour Bill, 1778, 3-35.

Panopticon: or the Inspection-House, 1791, 37-172. (Published with Postscripts published 1791 and Note.)

Panopticon *versus* New South Wales, 1802, 173-248.

A Plea for the Constitution, 1803, 249-84.
Draught of a Code for the Organization of Judicial Establishment in France, 1790, 285-304.
Bentham's Draught . . . compared with that of the National Assembly, 1790, 305-406.
Emancipate Your Colonies!, 1830, 407-18.
Jeremy Bentham to his Fellow-Citizens of France, 1830, 419-50.
Papers Relative to Codification and Public Instruction, 1817, 451-533.
Codification Proposal, 1822, 535-94.

Volume V

Scotch Reform, 1808, 1-53 + Tables.
Summary View of the Plan of a Judicatory, 1808, 55-60.
The Elements of the Art of Packing, 1821, 61-186.
'Swear Not At All', 1817, 187-229.
Truth *versus* Ashurst, 1823, 231-37.
The King *against* Edmonds, 1820, 239-51.
The King *against* Sir Charles Wolseley, 1820, 253-61.
Official Aptitude Maximized Expense Minimized 1830, 263-386.
A Commentary on Mr. Humphrey's Real Property Code, 1826, 387-416.
Outline of a Plan of a General Register of Real Property, 1832, 417-35.
Justice and Codification Petitions, 1829, 437-548.
Lord Brougham Displayed, 549-612. (Parts published 1831-2.)

Volume VI

Introductory View of the Rationale of Evidence, printed 1812, 1-187.
Rationale of Judicial Evidence, 1827, 189-585. (Text continued in Vol. VII.)

Volume VII

Rationale of Judicial Evidence (continued), 1-600.
General Index to Vols. VI-VII, 601-44.

Volume VIII

Chrestomathia, 1816-17, 1-191.
Fragment on Ontology, 192-211. (Based on MSS.)
Essay on Logic, 213-93. (Based on MSS.)
Essay on Language, 294-338. (Based on MSS.)
Fragments on Universal Grammar, 339-57. (Based on MSS.)

Tracts on Poor Laws and Pauper Management, 1797, 358-439.
Observations on the Poor Bill, 1797, 440-61.
Three Tracts Relative to Spanish and Portuguese Affairs, 1821, 463-86.
Letters to Count Toreno, on the Proposed Penal Code, 1822, 487-554.
Securities Against Misrule, Adapted to a Mahommedan State, 555-600.
  (Based on MSS.)

Volume IX

Constitutional Code, v-x, 1-662. (Parts published 1830-1.)

Volume X

Memoirs and Correspondence, 1-606. (Continued in Vol. XI.)

Volume XI

Index to Memoirs and Correspondence, i-iv.
Memoirs and Correspondence (continued), 1-170.
Analytical Index to the Works, i-cccxci.

Bentham's Theory of the Modern State

Introduction

Once again the modern state is under attack. Indeed, the modern state was born struggling. From the first the work of spreading the idea of the state was arduous, for its ideologists have had to win converts from competing ways of understanding the political world. The state had to meet and overcome the formidable aspirations of universalism. Initially it confronted the claims of the Church, and later the claims of Enlightenment universalism and its principal heir, socialism. The state met another challenger in parochialism. It had to conquer or conciliate the parochialism of corporations, and the even more powerful parochialism of peoples and cultures to whom all other men and institutions appeared simply alien or barbarian. Now, fresh contests with varieties of universalism and parochialism have made the survival of the state a pressing question for some. It is not that the existence of states is in immediate danger; statehood continues to be valued in practice. But the conduct of established states and the political development of others are no longer viewed with the same optimism that has marked thinking about the state since the sixteenth century. The optimism of earlier writers and state-builders can be accounted for only in part by their perception of the necessity of municipal governments, since this necessity is admitted now more than ever. Experiences of statelessness in this century have taught us as nothing else has that the lives and welfare of all men are bound up in practice with citizenship in a state. The contrast between this concession of the value of statehood in practice and earlier celebrations of the state idea is this: traditionally, no logical distinction was made between the state as a set of utilitarian institutions and the state as an ideal. As one writer expressed it, the state is not a fact at all but a myth; it is not a subject of political thought but a form of political thought.[1] The state idea has two cardinal

1

aspects, and together these give it its character and account for the enthusiasm with which it was embraced.

First, the state is inseparable from the notion of a single rationality higher than the changing and conflicting interests of individuals and groups. Faith in this higher rationality directed loyalty and obedience to the institutions in which it was expressed—to the person of the prince and later to a unified system of law. The particularity of the state is its second feature. Particularity has entailed recognition of the existence of a multitude of states. And it has meant that even states at war acknowledge that the enemy's conduct is rational when judged by the exigencies of its welfare and preservation. States can be restrained in their conduct toward one another only by mutual agreement or by superior force, in this view, for no higher rationality governs relations among states. At least, beyond the state there is no appeal. This characterization of the state describes a distinction between domestic and international affairs which continues to dominate both popular and scholarly political thought. The prevalence of this distinction is one sure sign that no substitute has been found for the state as a form of political thought. There is, however, no better indication of the loss of faith in the state idea than the view that this distinction between domestic and international relations—and the one between criminal and enemy which attends it—have ceased to be meaningful in practice, or worse, that they are misconceived.

I am by political preference an enthusiast of the modern state. If this enthusiasm is not reactionary or despairing of any other view of the political world, then the state must continue to have a claim on our loyalties, and the promise it held out to those engaged in state theory and state-building is of interest. Of these thinkers Jeremy Bentham meets the present need to reconsider that promise. He defended the state after the fiercest resistance put up by corporate privilege and religion to the consolidation of absolutism had ceased, and once the individualist basis of the state had been secured. He provided clear insight into the state as a legal entity, its ethical basis, and the institutions required for its support.

This book presents Bentham as a theorist of the modern state. He took up all of the principal themes of state theory—sovereignty, law as a way of exercising power, diplomacy and the relations of states, and toleration. And he recognized these as typically modern concerns. It may be that other theorists have given more thought to the peculiar character of modernity than Bentham, but none has been as preoccupied with modernization, or political development. None has proselytized more fiercely on its behalf. The proselytizing tone of Bentham's work is important;

for him the modern state was not an actuality that might be analyzed critically, but an aspiration. Modernization was an ideal. Although Bentham attended to techniques of state-building and to methods for overcoming resistance to modernization, his thought was not exclusively instrumental. The character of the modern state, he judged, was neither sufficiently understood nor sufficiently defended. He argued often for the practicability of the institutions he felt the state required, but Bentham's idea of the state cannot be comprehended simply by surveying his recommendations for institutional reform. For he also attempted to demonstrate what ideas made these institutions possible, or conceivable, at all. Here, the measure of Bentham's political thought is his view of the state rather than the impact of his programs on subsequent reforms, and his importance lies in his effort to reconcile men to politics by means of the state idea.

One thing is clear, Bentham was sensitive to the diversity and fragility of political order. The state's higher rationality does not overcome diversity, he insisted. The point of the principle of utility is precisely its claim that order is possible on the basis of the changing and conflicting desires of individuals and groups. Like other theorists of the modern state, Bentham assumed that diversity is inevitable, and assigned it positive value. He was equally convinced of the fragility of political order. Even men acting in good faith and in accord with the principle of utility may fail to achieve order or to maintain it, he admitted. Utility does not guarantee agreement. The reconciliation to diversity and fragility that Bentham proposed was not, therefore, an emotionally or aesthetically satisfying one. Romanticism was, after all, a perfectly comprehensible reaction against the rationality of the utilitarian state. The romantic attack persists because the longings for stability and common values that the state leaves unfulfilled persist. The satisfaction Bentham's state theory offered was purely intellectual. It explained the inevitability of diversity and fragility in modern politics. It promoted toleration of the one, and whatever solace insight can bring for the other.

Many of the concerns that inform my reading of Bentham's work are different from those that have governed other interpretations of his political thought. For one thing, the emphasis here is not on the origins and historical importance of Bentham's proposals for reform, as it was in Elie Halévy's wonderful study *The Growth of Philosophic Radicalism*.[2] Halévy's work is intellectual history at its best; he focuses on Bentham's youth and explores Bentham's alliance with intellectuals in the Enlightenment tradition. The ideas that most often characterize Enlightenment thought cannot by themselves illuminate Bentham's state theory, however. It is impossible to write about the state without sharing the concerns and making use of at least some of the ideas developed by "reason of state" thinkers. Strictly speaking, reason of state, called Machiavellism by its chief historian,[3] is a political doctrine associated with the period from the Renaissance to the consolidation of monarchical absolutism. More broadly, it is an enduring political attitude that takes the state as an ideal and accepts the imperatives this ideal generates. In this sense, it is an attitude Bentham shared and even encouraged.

The Enlightenment was characterized by belief in progress toward a cultural ideal—the rational self-development of individuals—and by belief that progress would be accompanied by universal and perpetual peace. Those Enlightenment thinkers who were not avowedly anarchistic in their aspirations nonetheless conceived of every order and association as chiefly educational. They thought of power and coercion as inevitably irrational. For some thinkers, power and coercion were impediments to intellectual culture, for others, they were at best the condition for intellectual progress. Although Enlightenment thinkers accepted the state as a fact, they were not resigned to it; their loyalties were cosmopolitan and they expected the state to be transcended by a world state or federation.

The chief characteristic of reason of state, by contrast, was that the doctrine took the parochial state as a norm and studied the consequences of doing so. Reason of state is inseparable from the idea of a public rationality, sometimes called utility, which could justify abrogating the restraints imposed on power by moral and positive law. Reason of state defended on principle deviations from the course of conduct recommended first by the universal church and later by the Enlightenment. The doctrine also rejected entirely the Enlightenment's notion of rulers as benevolent or tutorial figures. Instead, it accepted common egoism as the basis of rule and the personal power drives of rulers as the energy that got public business done.

Although the two traditions of political thought are opposed in this way, they do not appear in isolation; they cannot logically, for they require each other. Reason of state does not consist simply of prudence, or recommendations for setting aside law or morals in practice. The doctrine propounded a new basis for justifying opposition to other standards, standards which for a considerable period the Enlightenment provided. Similarly, the ambition of Enlightenment thinkers was to deny at least one assumption of reason of state: that the egoism of all men inevi-

4

tably slips into caprice and that power is therefore necessary. There are psychological reasons, too, why the traditions rarely appear in isolation. No matter how dedicated they are to the reformative powers of abstract principles, few thinkers can resist entirely the thrill of power; few lack an appetite for intrigue even though they despise the intriguers; few have not sought insight into the secrets of *arcana imperii* or taken their turn at the pleasurable calculations of diplomacy. Few thinkers, in short, would reject entirely the proud title political "insider," which is one of the marks of reason of state. Perhaps only Rousseau was more sensitive than Bentham to the peculiar relationship between rulers and intellectuals, or more disconcerting in his alternate abjurations of political ambition and claims to have political ties.

Bentham shared, then, many of the notions associated with reason of state. The mark of modern political practice, he insisted, is absolutism, and he knew that the state's ethical basis in individualism provided absolutism with a stronger justification and a broader field of exercise than ever before. No constitutionalist gave more thought to the necessity and justification of absolute power than Bentham, or cared more how to organize and exercise it than he. More important, Bentham propagated the notion of a higher rationality that he called utility. Utility's dictates, arrived at by "observation and calculation," take the form of exigencies and not choices. Utility ought to govern the actions of governors even though it is bound to conflict with the traditional demands of morality, with rights at positive law, and with the unrestrained inclinations of private men.

Bentham was also aware of the consequences of these ideas. There is no good without evil, he advised, and he directed rulers to prefer the lesser evil, as the phrase he came to use—"the greatest happiness of the greatest number"—suggests. In the same spirit, Bentham admitted the dark drives of political men and the difficulty of reconciling rulers to the demands of utility. His interesting work on the reward and punishment of officialdom shows that Bentham did not depend on either benevolence or the enlightened identification of interest between ruler and ruled to restrain the ruling few.

This is not to suggest that Bentham was a representative proponent of reason of state. He was concerned with the necessities of established (although imperfectly modernized) states engaged in regular and informed relations in a European state system. These circumstances alone account for the moderation that distinguishes him from earlier writers on the state. Nor did Bentham contribute anything to historicism or to the tendency to personify the state, which marked the later history of reason of state. Mention of this doctrine is not intended to prejudice the view of Bentham as an Enlightenment figure; it is appealed to, instead, to offset the emphasis Enlightenment studies ordinarily place on education and democratic institutions. Undeniably, Bentham adopted the formal aspects of continental rationalism and individualism. He manifested faith in progress and in the reformative powers of thought, and he was typically indignant at resistance to these. What is important is that in Bentham's mind progress was almost exclusively associated with the consolidation of the state and modernization of its institutions. Bentham never wavered in his assurance that utility's institutional expression was in the state conceived as a legal entity rather than in society simply. Because he did not share to the full his contemporaries' preoccupation with education, he did not conceive of the state as purely instrumental to the advance of culture. Bentham loathed the men who exercised power in practice, but he never kept intellectual culture and power apart or looked upon power as inevitably irrational. Politics could contain rationality, he showed, without becoming indistinguishable from education or social engineering.

Bentham turned his attention, then, to political matters that other writers of his time imagined would be transcended by progress or that they reluctantly abandoned to caprice. His lifelong concern for the organization, reward, and punishment of officials is one example. Another is his work on the relations of states. Despite their titles, and despite the hope of universal peace that is pronounced in these works, *Letters of Anti-Machiavel* and *Principles of International Law* admit considerations of reason of state. Not even the common interests of states and international law require philanthropy, or obviate calculations of the best interest of state, or proscribe war. Bentham adopted the Enlightenment's chief recommendation—publicity—even in the case of international affairs, but this did not mean that he rejected the main insight of reason of state. Public necessity, he contended, should be genuinely public. Insight into the exigencies of the state should not be restricted to rulers in the hope that public ignorance would ensure stability or in order to spare the public conscience. Bentham would force men generally to acknowledge the painful consequences of accepting the state as the norm of order.

This approach to Bentham's thought is also a departure from the questions ordinarily taken up by moral philosophers who have nearly monopolized Bentham studies. Often these ethical interpretations have obscured or trivialized the import of the principle of utility; they have invariably distracted readers from the purpose Bentham thought his principle would serve. In fact, barely a fraction of his work was on the subject of private morality; it is not the focus of *An Introduction to the Principles of Morals and Legislation* any more than it is the focus of Bentham's *Constitutional Code*. Private morality was always subordinate in his mind to the larger question of public utility. Whether the private and public recommendations of utility were different, as Bentham explained them, and whether they might conflict are not at issue here.[4] The point is that it was no abstract question of finding a standard for human relations, but the exigencies of authority that inspired Bentham's considerations. Sensitivity to political disorder and to the possibility of political reconstruction moved him, like others from the sophists to modern state theorists, to investigate the relation between morality and public necessity. Bentham produced the principle of utility for rulers precisely because of the inadequacy of traditional moral rules, benevolence, and even prudence to direct men engaged in public affairs.

The chief claim Bentham advanced for utility was as a rationale for legislation. The institutional expression of public utility was, for him, a unified system of law, and law was unquestionably Bentham's main concern. Jurisprudence, model codes, and legislative programs constitute the greater part of his writings. His singular interest in law is clear in the titles of his works, in the turn of his arguments, and in his own account of his efforts: he was famous, Bentham recorded, because he had superseded everything written before him on the subject of legislation. Before he wrote, the field of law was a "trackless wild"; his self-proclaimed "genius" lay here. The state was a legal entity, Bentham explained, because it was in a unified legal system that public utility was expressed.

Finally, this book does not join in the several attempts (not always performed in good faith) to fix Bentham's place on the spectrum radical-liberal-conservative. The extent of his democratic sympathies is still debated. It is agreed, however, that Bentham increasingly opposed some institutions, such as monarchy, and recommended others, such as parliamentary reform, and that taken together these political preferences earned him the title "radical." Bentham himself understood "radical" to be a purely partisan political distinction. Where his projects for reform are the subject of study, the chronology of Bentham's writings has been deemed critical, and using Halévy's work as a starting point, historians continue to investigate the circumstances that led Bentham to design and support radical programs. Some historians stress his association with

7

John Mill, the events of the French Revolution, or the efforts of Spain and Spanish America to resist Napoleon. Others emphasize motives, and argue that Bentham's political inconstancy was a self-interested reaction to political events, calculated to secure his codes a hearing in high places. This view is hostile not because it is false, but because it disparages these efforts at reform by making Bentham out to be a mere *"faiseur de projets"*; it denies him the noble failings characteristic of political men who exercise reason of state on behalf of their own utopian orders. Of course, Bentham's politics can be simply and charitably comprehended as one intellectual's problem of allegiance at a time when regeneration of the old regime was viewed with despair and construction of a new regime remained an aspiration. The point is that Bentham's change of political heart cannot be characterized as a theoretical change.

Bentham's view of the state, its ethical basis, and the principal institutions necessary for its support continued remarkably unchanged over the course of his long career. Where his state theory is the subject, chronology does not provide an organizing principle, and this book does not treat Bentham's writings successively. One thing is certain, the partisan title "radical" is of little use in studying much of his work, including much of his political thought. The contemporary attitudes Bentham opposed categorically were those he designated "aestheticism" and "asceticism." These attitudes, he contended, rather than disagreements over the advantages and disadvantages of monarchy, for example, were what made utilitarian legislation impossible.

If a single ideological stance can aid in understanding Bentham's work, it is that he was a self-conscious modern. More than any of his contemporaries who shared his emphasis on progress, Bentham rejected everything in the classical tradition of political philosophy. He diverged not only from classical metaphysics, but from classicism in all matters of subject and style. He abandoned Aristotle's classification of regimes (including mixed government) and the peculiar imperatives that govern each. He abandoned the notion of the best regime. He concentrated instead on individualism as the ethical basis of every modern political order and on the single rationality that is its accompaniment. Public utility and the legislation in which it finds expression were simply inconceivable, Bentham judged, without an understanding of knowledge and politics entirely different from the classical one. Bentham's notion of what constitutes modern legislation is the subject of Chapter 1.

1. A Utilitarian Code of Law:
Ordinary or Extraordinary Legislation?

> If we could suppose a new people, a generation of children the legislator finding no expectations already formed in contradiction to his views, might fashion them at his pleasure. (*TL,* 149)

Bentham expounded the principle of utility chiefly as a rationale for legislation. The political contest that brought life and meaning to this work was his struggle to reform English common law, and Bentham's most potent rhetoric was invariably directed at Blackstone and the legal profession. Utilitarian legislation had another opponent in classical political thought, and Bentham was equally unsparing in his attack on this tradition. In fact, his anticlassicism and his opposition to the English legal system sometimes converged, because of the connection he discerned between classicism and aristocratic politics. He was an enemy of aristocratic government, indeed of all regimes, including mixed government, and he substituted for regime the notion of a single rationality which the principle of utility prescribes. Bentham's main argument with classical political thought focused not on class rule, however, but on law. If utility is to serve as a rationale for legislation, then legislation itself must be made secure. That is, legislation must be acknowledged as the typical way of exercising power and social control, and lawmaking must be recognized as a continual process in response to diverse and changing desires that require adjustment. Legislation, in short, must be established as an ordinary and not extraordinary act. From this standpoint, Bentham's anticlassicism has importance apart from his attack on aristocratic government. His anticlassicism is in defense of an understanding of legislation which is clearly opposed to both the ancient view of law as custom and the ancient view of law as an instrument of education and character formation. Above all, ordinary legislation contrasts with the classical tradition of great Legislators, who more than anything else represent lawgiving as a unique and wonderful event.

Bentham was not the first to defend the ordinary character of legislation. Political theorists before him had described the modern state as a legal entity and law as the normal way of exercising power. Hobbes, for example, had written against the common law tradition, and insisted that the changeability of statute law is necessary for order. Still, there is more to legislation than releasing rulers from the established constraints of moral and positive law, Bentham knew; the principle of utility would transform public happiness and welfare from rhetorical phrases into concrete tasks. In any case, the work of vindicating legislation was not completed, for in the eighteenth century it faced a special challenge. A revival of code and constitution making had brought the classical image of the Legislator to prominence once again. Codifiers modeled themselves after ancient lawgivers, and every appeal to the classical image defied the claim that legislation is an ordinary act. At the same time, preoccupation with the educative effect of laws gave fresh force to the view that not only in its origin, but also in its purpose, law was antipolitical. Bentham was particularly sensitive to this revival of classicism, because he too styled himself the Legislator of his age. It was important for him to distinguish legislation from ancient lawgiving in order to make his theory of legislation comprehensible; it was also important as a personal matter for Bentham to distinguish himself and his work from ancient models. Bentham's effort to define the status of legislation is the subject of this chapter.

The intellectual company Bentham kept in his century was a company of humanists. In comparison with the thinking of two philosophers of the previous generation whom he particularly admired, Hume and Voltaire, the range of Bentham's thought was strikingly narrow. He cared nothing for history, for example, or aesthetics, and the title *An Introduction to the Principles of Morals and Legislation* misleadingly suggests that he gave equal attention to private morals and legislation. The literary style of Bentham's writings was similarly limited. Bentham's organization and language were idiosyncratic, and the tone of his writings was a curious mixture of logic and irony. The point is that these elements of style were as nearly as possible uniform throughout his work. In legal codes and political diatribes, Bentham spoke with the same voice, and deliberately so. For his peculiar restriction of subject and style reflects a determined rejection of everything classical. Bentham echoed the common boast of scientists, "our age is the oldest,"[1] and then went farther and discarded altogether, as other intellectuals of the eighteenth century did not, the classical standard of intellectuality.[2]

Classical thought conceived a dualism between knowledge and politics, and Bentham referred to this characteristic dualism when he complained that an opposition was generally supposed to exist between theory and practice. This opposition was a common legacy of classical thought, he lamented, and it tyrannized over his life and work. His anticlassicism found expression most often in fierce denials of any opposition between theory and practice, and he set himself the task of reconciling knowledge and politics in the field of law. Bentham's principal interest was not in the epistemological questions raised by the relation between theory and practice, however; he did not explore the origin of ideas or the special status of some ideas and their effect in the world. He endeavored only to define legislation, and the opposition between theory and practice assumed in his eyes a peculiar form. Bentham faced this tension each time he asked himself, as he did repeatedly: "What is the best way to be useful in legislation?"

If legislation is the political work of men of good character acting through institutions, then the way to be of use in the field of law is as a critic of institutions and counsellor to political men. Bentham's obvious enthusiasm for programs of reform, the rhetorical vein that runs throughout his writings (including the frequent charge of corruption), and his own assertions are all proof of the attraction politics had for him. "The only thing I ever did covet," he once wrote, was to be of use in ordinary "parliamentary business" (X, 233). Where success of his measures was the measure of merit, Bentham met only frustration and failure during his lifetime, and his influence on subsequent reformers and reforms is a matter of debate. But politics is only one answer to the question: "How to be of use?" Bentham also described himself to his patron, Lord Shelburne, as a "mongrel philosopher" who could and indeed would be of no use to the statesman in his parliamentary business (X, 245; I, 252). He devoted himself to speculation about the nature of a law and designed complete codes that illustrated his insights. At these times, Bentham's inspiration was the classical Legislator whose laws are the product of solitary wisdom. He even likened himself to Mentor, convinced as he was of his "genius" for legislation. Bentham's claim to "genius" is instructive; it indicates that the Legislator was supposed to be self-selected, and it allies the Legislator's work more to aesthetics than to politics. Indeed, to the extent that he looked on law as a Legislator's design, Bentham seemed to attach little importance to whether his codes would be adopted by despots or democracies. The Legislator, he knew, was an alternative source of law to political legislation. "Who should legislate?" was not, then, a simple matter of political preference for Bentham. It was more than just a question of the best form of government. Rather, "who should legislate?" posed a choice of Legislator or political men, knowledge or politics, as the source of laws.

No one was more sensitive than Bentham himself to this intellectual tension and its effects on his ambitions and political thought. "I have two minds," he wrote pointing to his divided nature,[3] "one of which is perpetually occupied in looking at and examining the other."[4] Not surprisingly, he suffered from considerable self-doubt. A sense of the "infirmity of human nature" preyed on him as he worked, and the state of his publications attests to it (I, iv). At least once he publicly recorded the disgust he felt for his own efforts, and he lamented over and over that the work he had done on this or that project was incomplete (I, i). It is also not surprising that Bentham's most fair-minded readers have hesitated to pronounce upon his "relative standing in the history of philosophy" or, for that matter, on his standing in economics.[5] The only one of Bentham's writings to enjoy a prominent and permanent place in the history of thought is *An Introduction;* the intellectual status of his work as a whole has been insecure, and with good reason.[6] Themselves heirs to the classical tension between theory and practice, Bentham's readers are certain that the standards that apply to works of philosophy are distinct from those that apply to political programs, and in many cases they are justifiably uncertain what Bentham's purpose in writing was. In this respect, his codes pose obvious interpretive difficulties. It is unclear whether Bentham meant them to be adopted by some foreign government or whether he mainly intended the codes to stand as criticism of actual laws. It is not evident whether he supposed them to have any philosophic content. In short, it is unclear how Bentham meant his codes to be "of use."

One thing is certain: when he attacked the notion "good in theory, bad in practice," Bentham was not merely protesting the resistance to reform that had caused his projects to be rejected. The attack was part of a larger effort to reconcile knowledge and politics in the field of law. This effort dominated his work. It resulted in what he aptly styled a "theory of legislation." And it sheds some light on his codes, which, like almost all of his writings, are an appropriate mix of the language of science—

logic—and of irony, that peculiarly political tongue. Bentham distinguished what was practical from what was "now practicable"; his codes were practical, he insisted, although adoption was not the only measure of their usefulness. The codes could be counted as failures if they were not imitated, but it was the logical relation of laws that they demonstrated as much as particular measures. The codes were meant to demonstrate to what extent legal security depends upon these logical relations and how far actual laws were from making men legally secure. The codes were important, then, as models of legislative form (V, 275). And they proved that a theory of legislation was practical. "In the Utopia of the sixteenth century," Bentham wrote, "effects present themselves without any appropriate causes; in this of the nineteenth century, appropriate causes are presented waiting for their effects" (V, 278). Bentham was convinced that a reconciliation of knowledge and politics was possible. In particular, he thought that he could point to a place for a Legislator and political lawmakers in the modern state. He did this by altering the classical understanding of both, if not more definitively than anyone before him, certainly with fewer regrets.

The idea that legislation is an extraordinary act has often been embodied in the figure of a great Legislator. Particularly when a new state is founded and new laws are wanted, or when old laws no longer inspire obedience and conflict reigns, political thought turns to the image of a Legislator. Underlying every such image are the desire for a new and stable order and the belief that someone with sufficient wisdom could design laws to unite men and secure their happiness. The Legislator is usually modeled closely after the ancient lawgivers Solon and Lycurgus; in every case, he is represented as a man of peculiar virtue and special knowledge who works alone and who may be a stranger to the place he remakes.

Bentham found the image of a Legislator personally appealing, although the Legislator was not someone he imagined might come, but someone he half-hoped to be. Through this image, he evidently reacted against the circumstances of his life. He compensated for the neglect and abuse he alternately felt he suffered at the hands of political men, and he assuaged the fear he shared with others that contemporary political institutions might fail to maintain legal order. Traditionally, the Legislator is more than an expression of personal disappointment and political despair, and according to even Bentham's recasting of the classical image, the Legislator embodies some positive idea of wisdom. Yet it is perfectly in keeping with the idea of a Legislator to see him first of all negatively,

13

as an alternative to politics. The classical Legislator always arrived to do the difficult work of political development or to repair political breakdown; he signified the fragility of political order and the reluctance men felt to reconcile themselves to fragility.

The classical Legislator presents a compelling image precisely because he does work alone and is an outsider. If he literally comes from afar, like Mentor to his island, the people are assured that he is absolutely neutral in their affairs, "without interest, connection, or dependence."[7] His laws are not only impartial, but also apolitical in their operation; they are conceived not as commands but as precepts for the improvement of those who abide by them, and they depend upon education or right beliefs, not coercion, for their effect (I, 467 and n.). The Legislator is alien above all by virtue of his peculiar understanding. His special wisdom may come from the gods or from philosophic reflection; in either case, he offers more than the good counsel of even the best practical politicians.[8] The Legislator knows better than the rulers and people of the place what laws are suitable for them and what form they should take, and he knows how men must be changed in order for these laws to be perpetually effected. Often, aesthetic terms are used to describe his work (he "designs" a code), and this language too is a mark of the Legislator's apolitical character; it conveys the ideal proportions of the order formed by his laws. It is eternally pleasing and complete. Since the Legislator's code is perfect, it cannot be improved, nor men made happier.

Bentham frequently portrayed himself as the Legislator of his age. He was a man of special virtue—at least the form selfishness took in him was benevolence (X, 95, 458; XI, 72). He might even become the "wisest and most *effectively benevolent* man that ever lived," for he trembled to realize that he had a genius for legislation.[9] More than once he contemplated designing a code for some foreign place, and imagined that like the Legislators of the past, whatever he gave for laws would be received as oracles (IV, 585; X, 458). But if Bentham sometimes thought of himself as a Legislator and of law as the product of his design, profound differences separated his from the classical conception. On this matter, Bentham was one of the first political thinkers to turn his back entirely on the ancients.

Bentham was not the only intellectual of his time to reject, or even to ignore entirely, the metaphysical basis of classical thought. But he was almost alone in his disdain for classical concerns. Like many of his contemporaries, he was powerfully influenced by Fénélon's romance *Telemachus*. Unlike them, however, everything classical that he read there excited his "contempt" (X, 11). Others were inspired by Mentor, the tutor of kings and molder of character; Bentham was interested in Mentor the lawgiver (and even so he thought the idea that the end of law is to generate virtue in men was pure sentimentalism). Indeed, the spectacle of utility defeated as a principle of legislation in that work was what started Bentham on his "career of life" (X, 10). Bentham used the image of the Legislator for his own purposes. He employed it simply to add force to his argument that laws are actually made by identifiable men, and not received or discovered; he thus ignored the religious basis of the classical Legislator's laws. And in direct contrast to the classical idea of a perfect and enduring order, he insisted that legislation must be continuously added to and changed. In everything that concerned the heart of the idea of the Legislator—his knowledge and the purpose of law—Bentham dismissed the classical view.

One difference between Bentham's Legislator and the classical model is striking. He gave no thought to the Legislator's personal qualities. Unlike Rousseau, for example, Bentham never longed for (and never longed to be) a paternal or godlike lawgiver. The Solons and Lycurguses, he knew, owed their titles to the love and reverence of the people, but he simply payed no attention to a modern Legislator's ability to inspire deep feelings (I, 467). Personality, he observed succinctly, was a "slender prop" for security (II, 586). More to the point, the Legislator was typically revered because he appears as a protector. He uses his knowledge to provide for and improve men, and they in turn feel directly and individually touched by him, as they would by a father or god who took care to create a place for each of them in his scheme. None of this mattered to Bentham because the law is not solicitous of men personally. "It is in the power of making men act by *class,*" he wrote, "that the strength of government consists" (III, 197). His Legislator issues only general rules, rules which apply to men individually but generally, and which aim at directing their conduct without changing their motives—without, that is, improving them. The Legislator need not, in short, appear as a paternal figure. Bentham often reversed the common political imagery which described the magistrate as tutor; the ordinary teacher and parent, he wrote, are deputies of the magistrate (I, 30).

Bentham did comprehend the emotional need men have for final judgment in the regulation of their affairs. He represented the judge, who brings the law to bear on men directly and individually, as a father figure. What interested Bentham, however, were not the sentimental aspects of a father figure that account for bonds of loyalty and trust, but those features that have to do with his mode of making decisions. The law court should resemble a domestic tribunal, he recommended, where everyone is present before the father-judge, who reconciles differences where possible and orders punishment where necessary (II, 47). The judge's decisions should be irrevocable, just as the classical Legislator's constitution was final and not susceptible to challenge, amendment, or change. Above all, Bentham allowed the judge complete discretion in coming to the truth of each case, for when the object is to prevent a failure of justice his judgment is better than any precedent or binding rule of procedure. Within the framework he devised for a highly legalistic and institutionalized state, Bentham left the judge unique freedom of decision. Of course, the judge remains an institutional figure; the Legislator is antiinstitutional. Still, Bentham's speculations on the domestic tribunal indicate that he understood the emotional and political necessity for someone with judgment and power to see that "a period is put to a cause" (*OLG*, p. 223). The judge pronounces only a legal decision, of course, and determines whether an injury has occurred and whether a man is criminal or innocent according to the law. He does not decide according to some metaphysical or psychological standard whether a man has the character of a guardian or laborer. But the judge's decision resembles the classical Legislator's to the extent that it turns on knowledge of what men deserve; his object is to put men in their proper place according to what is supposed to be a real, external standard. Neither Bentham's judge nor the classical Legislator needs to know what men want, for neither looks to satisfy men. In this, both judge and classical Legislator differ from Bentham's view of political lawmakers, whose aim in legislation is to secure expectations, and whose knowledge must consist precisely of the wants and circumstances of men.[10]

Traditionally, the force of the Legislator's personality is crucial to his mission, because he neither explains nor justifies his code. His laws are believed to be oracles and are accepted to the extent that he is revered. Where great Legislators issued laws, Bentham observed, the reason of the people was obsequious to the reason of a single man, and *ipse dixit* was literally the rule (I, 467). Bentham, however, opposed laws that were rhetorical or epigrammatic; in order to direct men's actions, laws must consist of many detailed provisions. Laws are specific and timely measures in response to specific instances of unhappiness (X, 552). And he objected to any law, however good, that owed its strength to its author's character. Laws should draw their strength solely from the reasons that accompany them, and these reasons should be the lawmaker's own. Briefly but pointedly, Bentham distinguished his position from that of ancient philosophers, denying that his work consisted of two distinct doctrines, one popular and one occult (I, iii).[11] He always opposed cheating men for their own good (I, 268). This matter of a rationale for law lies, of course, at the very center of Bentham's thought. His principle of utility is just that—a rationale for legislation (I, v). And utility depends upon effacing the distinction between popular and arcane. Utility rests on the acknowledgment of common sense.

Reasons for laws become important, Bentham explained, when it is accepted that laws must change (I, 102, 162). In the modern state, it is simply inconceivable that a Legislator would make himself useless by creating an unchanging order. This is what the classical Legislator does; he comes, speaks to the gods, issues oracles, and departs—leaving behind him a static regime. He represents lawmaking as an extraordinary act and permanence as an ideal. The Legislator in philosophy's greatest discussion of the subject conforms to this description; in Plato's *Laws,* he "calculates" to the end of general happiness, and the outcome of his calculation is that the 5,040 hearthfires remain forever the same.[12] Plato carefully distinguished the Legislator's code from codes whose framers draw up additional paragraphs as they find necessary.[13] The *Laws,* in short, describes the deliberate creation of a customary society which rests upon uniformity of belief and aims at preventing change.

Diversity and change, Bentham claimed, characterize modernity and the state. However much this is lamented by some, it cannot be undone. There is no fable to move men to live "in one single selfsame lifelong tone."[14] Rousseau shared Bentham's sensitivity to political fragility, and for him the Legislator's appeal was precisely that he represented the possibility of satisfying the longing for stability. Bentham, however, did not use stability or uniformity as ideals to criticize the modern world. Diversity and change are not corruptions of a perfect and unchanging idea; they come from man's nature. Bentham derived them from his understanding of happiness. No perfect happiness is possible, he wrote without regret, and with that broke entirely with the classical idea (I, 194). The modern state is a political order that takes as its aim the expression and satisfaction of changing and conflicting desires. The classical Legislator was a substitute for politics, but there can be no alternative to politics even as an aspiration, Bentham realized, if the state's rationality is based on desires that each man knows for himself. The knowledge political lawmakers need is information about these desires. It follows that knowledge of even the best code of laws does not improve men or make them especially fit for receiving or preserving some ideal constitution. Knowledge of the laws only makes obedience easier. Just two things are required of men in a world of constant flux, Bentham thought, honesty and habits of rule making and rule following (IX, 4-5). Utility as a standard for legislation is simply the way to take diversity into account and accommodate change.

No matter how much Bentham altered the classical idea of the Legislator, there were still times when the image of himself as a great lawgiver seemed to dominate his thought. In keeping with what has been said about the Legislator, Bentham's ambitions were excited when he judged that a place was entirely without any system of law. Where the institutions of modern states were absent, Bentham could imagine political development by design. And because the Legislator substitutes for politics, it often appeared to be a matter of indifference to him whether he would prescribe laws at the invitation of a despotism or a democracy.[15] In infant states, there are few expectations that new laws can disrupt, and Bentham seemed prepared to offer his services as the author of a complete code to Aaron Burr for his prospective empire in Mexico and to the new democracy in Greece. Similarly, if anarchy reigns, as it had when Lycurgus divided up Sparta's lands—when 10 secure acres were better than 1,000 insecure ones—Bentham's code would be of use (I, 318). Thus, he praised the French code, despite its many defects, as an improvement on the preceding chaos (IV, 500). Bentham sometimes suggested that English common law was not law at all, and when he did he exposed his fear of crisis at home. He knew better, however, and agreed with Cromwell that England was no "clean paper" (IV, 501).[16] As revealing as his ambition to be a Legislator is the fact that Bentham never did draw up a code and send it to some foreign place, not even when solicited.[17] The code he sent to Greece was not his own; he had never even read it (IV, 584-585).

There is no reason to think that Bentham despaired of legislating for a people solely because he was afraid that his codes would be rejected. Nor was he deterred by difficult considerations of how to mold men's characters and beliefs; education was not the end of law. Insofar as there is an intellectual reason for his restraint, it is his judgment that new laws disrupt expectations. Consideration of the "influence of time and place on legislation" reveals that at least a feeble kind of expectation exists everywhere (I, 180; IV, 409, 561). Only in the eyes of "an English capitalist" is Mexico a land of "utter darkness" (II, 569). An alien Legislator cannot tell whether new laws secure or disrupt expectations; a veritable army of legislators and administrators is required to perform the "statistic function" of gathering local information about expectations (I, 180-181). Since Montesquieu wrote, Bentham explained, the number of documents that a legislator would require has been enlarged, for the lawmaker must lay open the whole tenor of a people's life and conversation, paint the face and geography of their country, and have a minute view of their present laws, manners, and religion (I, 173). Like Rousseau, Bentham understood laws as reflective of the state of a people, rather than as pedagogical. He had little confidence that legal security could be achieved in infant states that had "received" laws: "The constitution of a state is one thing," he cautioned with regard to new states in particular, "the conduct of the government and of the people under the constitution, another thing" (II, 568). This is not to say that the codes Bentham produced were a waste; he did think them useful if they served as models of legal form. In this way, Bentham left himself something of the Legislator's role.

Only once did he design and promote a new order as if it were "now practicable." That was the Panopticon prison plan, and Panopticon is surely one source of the popular characterization of Bentham as Legislator. The aesthetic inspiration for Panopticon is documented. It originated in his brother's novel, circular design, and as he developed ideas for its use, Bentham seemed to be following Mentor's advice to "reduce everything to a frugal and noble simplicity."[18] Where Panopticon was concerned, he abolished all established institutions in his mind and, he regretted later, ignored politics. His intention was to transform the prison institution and by doing so to reform its most malignant inhabitants. In all this, Bentham acted the Legislator. Even here, however, he set out the principles by which Panopticon could be managed and modified; he did what in his view any modern Legislator must to make himself truly useless—see that his scheme is reformable (X, 269). His rage at the rejection of the Panopticon plan can be charged in part at least to the committee's claim that his scheme was "too exceptionable on general grounds . . . to be adopted from confidence in an individual" (XI, 149-150; III, 303; II, 420). For Bentham had labored to promote Panopticon as something more than a projector's curious product and to make its benefits clear and accessible. The chief point here is that Panopticon was a practical design for an institution—a prison, school, factory, or workhouse—and no more. It was not a microcosm of a state, and Bentham did not use it to criticize actual states. If the prisoners housed there seemed to have been set strangely apart from one another, this had to do

19

with the conditions for repentance; Panopticon was not meant to serve as a model of anomic or authoritarian relations generally. In any case, the inspector in Bentham's plan regulated his charges by means of punishment rather than by the insensible effects of personal example, and there is a world of difference between restrained, even repentant, criminals and a race of virtuous men. Bentham had no patience with "political romances" (I, 533) or "wild projects of regeneration" (X, 233).[19] He had no intention of providing a site for testing metaphysical propositions or experimenting with character formation. Indeed, he feared that Panopticon would be misinterpreted in just this way and operated by men who sought to impose their tastes on others "unembittered by contradiction" (IV, 65). Bentham called both educators and political men who wanted to create a uniform order despotic. He was simply not interested in even the idea of a perfect order, or in teaching men to think of it.

The image of himself as a great Legislator constituted only one side of Bentham's divided thought and self-image. On the other side, he often discussed lawmaking as a political, specifically parliamentary process. In the modern state, he advised, laws must be made by legislators and administrators, by political insiders who are different in every way from the Legislator. The Legislator is independent and alien; the political insider is dependent and familiar. Political men, Bentham wrote, beg and ask secrets (X, 233). He was eager to claim ministers and political aspirants as confidants, and thus claimed for himself and his work some intimate relation to political lawmaking—another affair entirely from the Legislator's lawgiving.

Political men cannot exercise total discretion and do not act alone, Bentham knew. Dependence and gratitude are the twin ties that bind the political fraternity, be it court or parliament, and require its members to act together and through institutions (V, 564). The "clue to the interior of the labyrinth" reveals not only the action of the "principle of self-preference," but also the inevitability of political fraternization and institutionalization (X, 80). These marked the democratic order he proposed in *The Constitutional Code* as they had court or aristocratic Parliament. Moreover, political men cannot make laws without attending to what the people want. The Legislator need only speak; he issues oracles and departs. Political men must listen; they remain behind. Bentham's principle of utility is a political rationale for law precisely because it directs lawmakers to listen (I, v). Its peculiar excellence as a standard for legislation is that it enables legislators to listen better than ever before, and the result is a greater chance of stability, or at least a better likelihood of predicting disagreement and disorder. What legislators hear is that laws must change but that total change is impracticable, since even the best new laws may disrupt expectations. "Hot headed innovators, full of their own notions, only pay attention to abstract advantage. They reckon discontent for nothing," Bentham wrote (I, 181). Not so political legislators. Their aim is always peace or, more exactly, the settlement of current disorders. If they follow the principle of utility, they may increase "positive good" as well. But utility's import is principally negative, as the next chapter explains; its aim is security, or minimizing disappointment.

Bentham's notion of politics was also distinct from the classical view, then. Classical politics was an expression of character, while politics in Bentham's thought has nothing to do with the character of men, and laws are not instruments of education or character formation. Indeed, the very idea of character loses its meaning where there is no regime but only a world in flux. On this point, Bentham's peculiar reading of *Telemachus* is once again illuminating. He thought that the whole point of Fénélon's simple, didactic work—that the end of law is to generate virtue in subjects—was pure sentimentalism (X, 11). Although he called Telemachus his "model of perfect virtue," outside of romances the virtues of the ancient Greeks and Romans were more than offset for him by the enormity of their crimes. They treated other men as beasts, he wrote (II, 537). Whenever ancient virtue was raised as a standard, Bentham reminded his readers of slavery and of the "war-admiring turn" of their histories (II, 544; *Correspondence,* II, 145-149). His youthful attraction to Telemachus was erotic, he explained in retrospect; he envied him sleeping with Eucharis. Bentham reduced the virtues to honesty and benevolence, and then refused to make even benevolence a criterion for political men. He simply allowed no part for character in politics, which is why the role of Mentor as tutor, so attractive to his contemporaries, meant nothing to him. Diversity and change, those marks of modernity, led Bentham to reduce knowledge to information. They also inspired him to reduce character to responsibility (I, 268). He found a substitute for character in the notion of responsible behavior, often connected with professionalism.

What remains of the Legislator, given Bentham's view of political lawmaking? A sort of knowledge that he called metaphysics does have a place in his discussion of law, and Bentham believed that if knowledge and politics, Legislator and legislation were properly understood, they could be reconciled. The material expression of this accommodation was a code of law like the ones he drew up. For this reason too, and not only because he harbored a passion for classification per se, codes played a profound part in Bentham's work. A modern legislator might design a model code—an anatomy or plan for a body of law—whose measures could be adopted and amended by politics. Politics can produce good laws and political men can even pronounce good reasons for their laws, Bentham reflected, but only a code can give rational form to laws where none existed before. A code can make known "the true nature and mutual connections" of laws (*OLG*, p. 234). The knowledge a modern Legislator brings to lawmaking comprehends these universal, unchanging, and purely formal connections. Codification is actually a matter not of metaphysics, therefore, but of logic. "The science of law," Bentham wrote, is "the most considerable branch" of "the logic of the will" (I, iv). He hoped to do for laws, which he designated expressions of a sovereign will, what Aristotle had done for statements of understanding— demonstrate that laws as well as statements can stand in logical relation to one another. He would demonstrate the "natural and universal principles" on which a body of law is grounded (*OLG*, p. 232) and set out a "universal anatomy of the entire body of the law" (*OLG*, p. 308n.). Although the science of law was still in its "cradle," Bentham meant his understanding of formal relations to open up the hitherto "trackless wild" of legislation (*OLG*, p. 232). He stated his purpose dramatically: "O logic!—born gatekeeper to the Temple of Science[s], victim of capricious destiny! doomed hitherto to be the drudge of pedants! come to the aid of thy great master, Legislation" (X, 145).

This work on codification promised only formal gains in the field of law, but these were not negligible. A good code ensures that the content of laws will be good insofar as content is affected by "want of amplitude and discrimination . . . indeterminateness, contradiction, tautology, ambiguity, and obscurity" (*OLG*, p. 310). Nowhere are these formal qualities more important than where laws are concerned, Bentham insisted. It is not enough that all the world acknowledge theft as evil; the cases in which taking the goods of another constitute theft depend upon the laws (I, 161-162, 193). Nothing matters more to the lives of men than that each law define a class of act considered to be an offense, that this law be distinguishable from every other law, and this class of act from lawful acts. Indeed, Bentham sometimes claimed that "with a good method, we go before events," and that if not every individual offense, at least every species of offense could be foreseen because it could be deduced from the code (III, 205-206; *OLG*, pp. 164-165). For the most part his claims were stated more modestly; if it expresses the logical relation of laws, a code ensures that the body of law is comprehensive and non-contradictory. "To be without a *code,*" he judged, "is to be without justice" (X, 597). His chief dissatisfaction with current codes was that they were incomplete (III, 206).

Bentham's use of the phrase "body of law" was not carelessly anthropomorphic (I, 163; *OLG,* p. 308n.). The body serves as our most familiar image of a whole, and he hoped that his codes would be complete and require nothing outside themselves to be understood. In this one sense Bentham meant his codes to be educative, for those subject to them should be able to know the law without an intermediary's assistance (V, 236). His codes, like codes everywhere, were meant to provide greater legal security than the old system by doing away with "technical," or "lawyer's," law. Sometimes Bentham went so far as to promise that a utilitarian code would be self-enforcing, for there would be no dispute about what the law is; the law should need no interpretation (III, 207). A code is the only weapon against "judicial legislation," he wrote; a code will "guard the guardians" (X, 597). Where Bentham was not doing battle directly with common law, however, he gave a less restricted account of the judiciary's role, and admitted that even the best codes require interpretation, that is, judicial lawmaking. If the metaphor "body of law" is taken to mean more than comprehensiveness and noncontradiction, and to point in addition to the autonomy of law, it is misleading. For Bentham was interested not only in codes per se, but also in legal systems and the imperatives they generate. He was interested, that is, in the political apparatus necessary to give law effect. His logic of the will was addressed to, and not against, the legal profession.

The Legislator's special knowledge, then, is logic. His distinctive part in lawmaking is to pronounce formal rules, rather than particular measures. He lays down "universal and unchanging connections" whose purpose is to assure a complete and noncontradictory body of law; their purpose is not to provide a permanent antidote to political instability (as was the case with the classical Legislator's rules). Nor does Bentham's Legislator work alone; it requires politics to give content to laws, and this content continually changes. In short, Bentham does not use the idea of the Legislator to represent lawmaking as an extraordinary act. It remains to say that insofar as he emphasized the formal character of the Legislator's contribution to lawmaking, Bentham avoided as nearly as possible a dilemma that plagued other code and constitution makers of the eighteenth century. Traditionally the Legislator is self-selecting, and because of his peculiar status, his code is received. Its acceptance has nothing to do with general agreement. This aspect of the Legislator was a common feature of other eighteenth-century lawgivers who took on themselves the classical image; there was some danger that the Legislator image would conflict with the enlightened, and especially the republican, values they commonly espoused. By contrast, the self-selecting character of Bentham's Legislator was not at all in conflict with his prescriptions, so long as these were principally formal.

According to Bentham, a Legislator would provide a model code which follows the strictures of the logic of the will, but it remains for politics to produce laws. Codification, he knew, says nothing about the content of laws or about the political process that produces them. It says nothing about the political values laws serve. His recommendations for codification, Bentham conceded, could be applied to common law. But it was the idea of a code whose content is deduced from the principle of utility that preoccupied him. The principle of utility directs all of the reasons given for laws to "a single center," he wrote (I, 162). New laws can be made and old ones changed, but these must be referred back to utility. Where content is concerned, utility replaces the Legislator in the modern state. Of course, utility is a formal principle. It does not point to any particular content for laws; it simply indicates what political legislators must consider. The knowledge needed by these lawmakers in determining how an act stands with respect to utility is not philosophic understanding but information about men's desires. Where knowledge is reduced to formal principles and information, and politics to the expression and satisfaction of desires—just as Bentham asserted—the two do not conflict.

The content of utilitarian legislation has been described as "sublimated common sense."[20] Indeed, Bentham hoped that the laws would correspond quite literally to common sense, but unsublimated common sense: "The goodness of the laws depends upon their conformity to general expectation," he wrote (TL, p. 148). Law should take what men know in common as its basis, social expectations. Utility's radical character comes from the attention it pays to expectations not previously accorded legal recognition. Utility therefore excludes both blind routine and everything arbitrary. It ignores both philosophic insight into true happiness and purely personal sentiment. Even so, Bentham admitted that utility could not guarantee peace and happiness. Expectations may be irreconcilable. In his view, however, the worst enemy of utilitarian legislation was fanaticism, for it made utilitarian adjustments not only impractical but also inconceivable. Utility cannot combat fanaticism because it has nothing to offer to those for whom fanaticism has appeal. But utility can identify fanaticism. It can expose opposition to legislation which is purely rhetorical, for utility alone points to "clear and determinate objects" as the basis for legislation. The strongest claim Bentham made for utility is this: it is the best chance for legal security in the modern state (I, 161; II, 291).

Bentham believed that a utilitarian code could reconcile knowledge and politics in the field of law. He attempted a personal reconciliation of Legislator and politician as well. The image of himself as a Legislator evoked ambivalent sentiments in Bentham. He knew from experience that the genius, the independent outsider, was from another view the dependent and even the victim of political men. He was "dangerous" (I, 246) to existing institutions, but he requested a "certificate of harmlessness" (X, 441); countries would take what he gave them for oracles, but he was "ashamed of an unrecognized existence" and felt "like a cat or a dog that is used to be beaten by everybody it meets" (X, 26). An apology Bentham sent to Lord Shelburne equals anything Rousseau wrote as evidence of the conflict between defiance and dependence: "Being a sort of mongrel philosopher . . . you must allow me to snarl at you a little, now and then, while I kiss the beautiful hands you set to stroke me" (X, 245).

One way to mitigate the mixed and unhappy condition of the outsider would have been to gather disciples among political men and speak through them. Whatever intellectual historians have thought of philosophical radicalism as an influential movement, by his own admission Bentham was a failure in the role of spiritual father; he turned on his sons. He accused John Lind of stealing a manuscript (I, 247) and his "grandsons" fared no better. Ricardo had not the courage to cite him (X, 498) and Brougham had no courage at all (X, 588). Bentham must have thought he had come to the identical state he had witnessed Lord Shelburne arrive at politically—the state of Colossus with head of gold and legs of clay: "below the head, there is not a grain of reputation to be found" (X, 236).

Bentham eventually fashioned a self-image suitable for one who had spent his life "as much above party in one sense as . . . below it in another" (X, 386), an image that combined the intellectual status of the outsider with some of the personal satisfaction of the political insider. "I am," he wrote in one description of his efforts, "the unpaid . . . informer" (III, 509). The image of the informer fascinates because it suggests the ability to exist simultaneously in two opposing worlds. For Bentham, it meant that he could claim to enjoy the insider's confidence of ministers and share their knowledge not of books but of men (V, 587n.). The hare could use the hunter's weapons; he could attack motives and brandish rhetoric. Indeed, Bentham boasted he had surpassed political men at their own game. One of his greatest personal triumphs was outdoing Shelburne by uncovering the nefarious course of British diplomacy on the continent in *Letters of Anti-Machiavel* (X, 212). Above all, armed with the principle of utility, he could sense the political winds more keenly than political men, could "listen" better (XI, 9-10). Bentham thereby exacted his revenge for the neglect of his programs. At the same time, he enjoyed an even more important ability. He understood the character of law in the modern state and the form it must take to achieve its purposes. That understanding was his great work. His "genius" was not simply that he could recommend reforms but that he could explain the principle of reform in general and the language and legal form these measures must take. This work was possible, he satisfied himself, precisely because he was an outsider, and Bentham meant outsider in a purely psychological sense. He took it as a general rule that only those "oppressed with their insignificance" are moved to perform the "ardent and persevering" labor of thought (II, 249).

Bentham's distance from all thought that takes the classical heritage as its standard is revealed by this remark. All that is left is the labor of thought; its aims are instrumental. Logic and information between them divide the realm of knowledge, and they are, as Bentham had insisted, reconcilable with politics. In the modern state, they are at the service of legislation to satisfy desires. In all this, Bentham defended the ordinary character of legislation. And with legislation secure, it was necessary to set out the individualist psychology that would provide its ethical basis and explain its force. This is the subject of Chapter 2.

2. A Social Psychology for Legislators

> Happiness is a very pretty thing to feel, but very dry to
> talk about. (IV, 64)

Bentham distinguished legislation both from law as the foundation of an ideal and unchanging order and from law as an instrument of character formation. Legislation should be understood instead as a special way of accommodating individuals' desires—as an expression of utility. Utilitarian legislation is, in this view, a higher rationality that stands above the changing and conflicting interests of men.[1] This having been said, two tasks remain if legislation is to be understood, and Bentham performed them both with the help of arguments drawn from psychology. He used psychology to set out the ethical basis of laws that take desires for their content; in particular, he used psychology to demonstrate that the proper end of laws (and of the state as a legal entity) is to secure expectations. He also appealed to psychology to explain the force of law, or the operation of punishment. Together, these two discussions occupy central place in the great part of Bentham's many legal writings.

Bentham's appeal to psychology was not exceptional; in the eighteenth century, political thought was firmly and self-consciously rooted in psychology. This psychology, the proud child of natural science, has been suitably named naturalism. Bentham opened *An Introduction* with a classic statement of naturalism:

Nature has placed mankind under the governance of two sovereign masters, *pain* and *pleasure*. It is for them alone to point out what we ought to do, as well as to determine what we shall do . . . They govern us in all we do, in all we say, in all we think: every effort we can make to throw off our subjection, will serve but to demonstrate and confirm it. In words a man may pretend to abjure their empire: but in reality he will remain subject to it all the while (I, 1).

Naturalism is not a unified doctrine, though, and ordinarily the psychological theories that go under that name are distinguished by the relative autonomy they assign reason in directing or moderating the passions. Where Bentham is concerned, however, psychological doctrines are more usefully distinguished by their general character than by their detailed accounts of mental operations. Briefly, one focus belonged to a psychology of learning, which explained the origin of ideas and the workings of the understanding. A quite different focus belonged to social psychology, which provided an analysis of men's inclinations and the actions that follow from them in order to predict social relations. Bentham borrowed widely from both sorts of psychological theory for his own purely legalistic purposes.

In the eighteenth-century view, not only could nature be known, but the term "nature" was meant to include all that men can know, and the study of nature was thus inseparable from epistemology. Psychology was made to serve epistemology by inquiring into the origin of ideas, and naturalism has been succinctly characterized as a "historical" psychology.[2] It traced thoughts and actions back to the motives—the pleasures and pains—which according to different views either occasioned or caused them. And it traced these sensations to the external circumstances by which they were excited. Locke's *Essay concerning Human Understanding* was the standard work on naturalism, and succeeding developments, especially in epistemology, proceeded from that text. Locke's efforts and those of his successors aimed not only at acknowledging the sovereignty of pleasure and pain which Bentham pointed to, but also at reconciling men to it. And these efforts were successful; in an era passionately opposed to absolutism of every sort, it is remarkable that Bentham's words and countless others like them were so rarely a cause of lament. The reason is clear, though. This new insight into the workings of the mind and the origin of ideas was satisfying because it could be employed as a weapon against dogma and authority generally. Psychology's most vaunted victory was, of course, the possibility of enlightenment and the promise of intellectual autonomy. In its most radical version, a historical psychology of learning promised that men could become entirely equal and sympathetic. Bentham had no quarrel with aspirations for intellectual autonomy or with psychology's use as a weapon against enlightenment's enemies. These efforts were not his main interest, however. Instead, he appealed to the historical method that psychology taught in order to explain to political men the operation and force of laws. His theory of punishment depended upon a historical psychology. Bentham's debt to Lockean psychology, and his departures from it as well, are the subject of the first section below.

Locke's *Essay* was the starting point for investigations into the origin of ideas and the operation of the understanding. His work did not deal with the bearing one man's pleasures and pains had on those of other men; certainly, the principles of this relationship could not be found there. This is the business of social psychology, which takes up where Lockean psychology, strictly speaking, does not go. Bentham never claimed that his interest in psychology was epistemological, but nothing indicates his alliance with those who tried to use psychology to explain and even predict social relations better than his emphasis on will rather than understanding, and his conclusion that security is man's chief desire and the great end of law. Bentham was not the first to thread his way between the several investigations psychology opened up. Helvetius had gone this path before him, and Bentham seemed to value this intellectual apprenticeship above any other. Helvetius first modified Locke's historical psychology, and then put his conclusions to use in a critical study of ideas as a way of exercising power and in a political history of its exercise. Bentham learned psychology from Locke's successors—not by reading Locke directly. He thus encountered psychology in its most extreme sensationalist version, used by Helvetius to describe past authority as a form of victimization and to support radical egalitarianism. As ardent an admirer of Helvetius as he was, Bentham did not share Helvetius's vision. Bentham was committed to political authority, and he accepted the coercion and inequality that accompany all political order. It is not enough, he thought, to show that political relations are oppressive, or even to indicate the ideological means and historical course of that oppression. Psychology must be used to provide a standard for regulating social relations. Despite its power to combat the forces opposed to reform, Helvetius's social psychology was wholly inadequate as a rationale for reform, legislative reform in particular. For this, Bentham needed his own social psychology, as the second section below explains.

Bentham had nothing particularly new to say on the subject of psychology. What is of interest is the way he borrowed from the doctrines of his day and used psychology for his own peculiarly legalistic purposes.

He did not contend that the political purposes psychology was commonly made to serve were wrong. It was used to explain the origin and limits of political authority and to show the possibility of intellectual independence from authorities—clerical authorities in particular. Bentham applauded both ends. He certainly accepted the view that satisfaction of the desires of individuals ought to be the measure of every relation between ruler and ruled. And he enlisted psychology in uncovering intellectual oppression, including the deliberate manufacture of superstition by men in power—though the enemy in his eyes was less the clergy than the legal profession. It is equally plain, however, that Bentham thought work in these two areas was largely completed and did not require his full attention. When he took up questions of authority and obedience in *A Fragment on Government,* he did not have to defend individualism as the ethical basis of rule; his antagonist was Blackstone, who accepted individualism, Bentham argued, but failed to apply it consistently as a political standard. Similarly, when he attacked the Church of England, it was as one element of the conservative political establishment. The administration of oaths, he charged, encouraged habitual insincerity. He did not have to wrestle with faith itself, as continental radicals had to in their enthusiastic battle against clericalism. Bentham's passion was reserved for lawyers who deliberately created superstition and enjoyed superstition's inevitable product—obsequiousness. He wanted to expose and reform the legal profession, but he did not want to do away with lawyers' power entirely, and unlike Helvetius, he did not want to substitute a new leadership of intellectuals in their place.

What distinguishes Bentham's use of psychology is that he was perhaps the first political thinker since Locke to address himself to, and not against, political men. The arguments he constructed with psychology have to do with the purpose of law (securing expectations), the range of the legal system given this purpose, and its operation. His audience was legislators, and his work on this subject more than any other was didactic as well as critical. The best evidence for this is rhetorical: where the purpose and force of law were at issue, Bentham used the simplest and most effective rhetorical device—repetition. Accordingly, this chapter draws from a number of his writings on civil law and punishment.

Bentham's Reading of Lockean Psychology

Bentham lauded Locke as the "first master of intellectual truth," but admitted that he read the *Essay* as a duty, because it was spoken of highly. He complained that Locke's "fictitious entities such as power" puzzled him. He bowed to Locke because without him "those who have taught me would have been as nothing," referring to the authors of radical sensationalist psychology, especially Helvetius, who had modified Locke's work, leaving no place for Locke's troublesome "power" (X, 22, 142). Their efforts resulted in the psychology that Bentham drew on for *An Introduction* and his other work on civil law and punishment.

Locke's declared ambition had been to search out the "true history of the first beginnings of human knowledge."[3] He described pain and pleasure as movements toward and from continual states of uneasiness. Pleasure is not distinct from pain in this account, in fact these might be called relief and privation. And no satiation is possible in this view. Locke's vision of sensations held true for the thoughts that follow on them as well. "It is a contradiction to the natural state of childhood for . . . [youths] to fix their fleeting thoughts," he wrote;[4] indeed, all ideas change in a continual succession, and men do not seem to think long on any one thing. Locke's psychology presented a dilemma that would haunt every student of mental operations. Men are, by this description, subject to the tyranny of present uneasiness; they seem to be sufferers of spontaneity and insatiety. But business of all sorts, moral and intellectual business included, requires attention. Locke was certain that in practice this dilemma was only an apparent one, for he wrote that uneasiness was the "chief, if not only spur to human industry and action."[5] The *Essay* explained how it is that men avoid being the victims of uneasiness, of fleeting desires. Sensation is only one of two sorts of mental experience, Locke thought; the other is reflection.[6] Sensations are only the occasion and the material for other, independent mental operations. The mind can multiply thoughts; it can also create them.[7] Men can choose to gratify or deny the solicitations of uneasiness, and they can even make ideas more or less pleasing to themselves.[8] The mind, in short, is not simply subject and passive. By "power," by a special sort of mental effort, men can "suspend" themselves in a state of uneasiness, forbear responding to the claims of uneasiness, and engage in a "fair examination" of what they ought to do in pursuit of happiness.[9] Locke's psychology is no ascetic's vision. Because sensations are both the occasion and the material for our thoughts and actions, the acquisition of rich and various sensational experiences must be of value. Simply, forbearance and foresight are necessary for happiness. They are the evidence of reason at work, of morality itself. Locke's psychology culminates in a didactic recommendation not of self-denial but of self-control.

Locke's resolution of this psychological dilemma inspired revisionism by many distinguished successors who charged that the *Essay* did not provide a completely consistent psychology. Although Locke had made the sensational material of ideas clear, he had left unexplained independent faculties of the mind, internal experiences. These must be similarly reduced to their origins. Helvetius was the most radical in his search for a purely sensationalist psychology which would combine sensation and reflection.[10] All mental operations are transformed sensations, he asserted. "All judgments are no more than pronouncing upon sensations experienced."[11] There are no independent faculties to lift men past the solicitations of uneasiness. Pleasure and pain are not merely the occasion for thought and action; they actually produce it: "Corporeal sensibility is the sole cause of our actions, our thoughts, our passions, and our sociability."[12] Helvetius still had to account for the fact that some sensations affect men while others pass unnoticed, and for this purpose he introduced the notion of "attention." "Attention" is no improvement on Locke's concepts of power and reason; indeed, it is not so much an alternative to Locke's ideas as it is a denial of the problem Locke posed and then resolved in the *Essay*. For "attention" signifies a radical and uncreative egoism from which there is no escape. With his notion of "attention," Helvetius apparently refused to attribute any moral or political significance to Locke's crucial distinction between short-term and long-term interest—between pleasure and happiness. Bentham echoed the problem Helvetius had pretended to resolve when he observed that "we experience without cessation a variety of sensations which do not interest us, and which glide by without fixing our attention" (*TL*, p. 20); he echoed radical sensationalism's circumvention of the problem when he decided simply to call the pleasures and pains that do cause thought and action "interesting perceptions" (I, 17).

Bentham was acquainted with the work of another of Locke's successors, Hartley, who also explored mental history. Where Helvetius wrote of "attention," Hartley developed the principle of the habitual association of ideas. Hartley's psychology was based on an elaborate mechanistic theory of motions according to which external objects set up tiny vibrations in the nerves and the brain. The repetition of vibrations leaves "vestiges" in the brain's medullary substance, and produces the association of objects and ideas in the mind.[13] "Each action," he concluded, "results from previous circumstances of body and mind, in the same manner, and with the same certainty, as other effects do their mechanical causes."[14] Hartley was satisfied that this theory proved how comple-

32

mentary were man's actions and the course of nature; God moves men, and habitual association is the mechanism by which they will become increasingly equal and sympathetic. Bentham shared neither Hartley's interest in mental processes nor the conviction Hartley held along with all who anticipate paradise that the harmony of interests means the identification of interests—uniformity.[15] Nonetheless, Bentham found Hartley's principle of association useful, for it lent the authority of science to his idea that men are influenced most by habitual expectations, an idea that was critical to his theory of legislation. He was careful, of course, to observe that, strictly speaking, a habit is indistinguishable from the acts and perceptions by which it is formed, and cannot itself be the cause of anything. But he was happy to leave these epistemological subtleties to the experts: "The enigma . . . may be satisfactorily solved upon the principle of association, of the nature and force of which a very satisfactory account may be seen in Dr. Priestley's edition of Hartley on Man." For his purposes, Bentham was content to accept the influence of habit as a "matter of fact . . . not readily accounted for" (I, 57).

Bentham cited current developments in psychology, then. More important, he understood quite well the limited usefulness of historical psychology for his own work. Psychology is "mental physiology," he explained (II, 478). It is a science called dynamics whose subject is just what his title said it was: the *Springs of Action* (I, 205-206). Psychology considers pleasure and pain in the character of means or causes (I, 11). The details of this operation were never Bentham's main concern, however. He did not worry over the much-debated question whether a motive is an idea of pleasure or pain, or the pleasure or pain that accompanies an idea; these seemed to him to be "mere questions of words," and their solution "immaterial" to his purpose (I, 47n., 207, 211). He took the term motive in its "most extensive sense" as anything that can contribute to give birth to, or prevent, any kind of action (I, 46).[16] The pleasures of honor were propagated by a "peculiar sympathy" among relatives and friends, Bentham observed, but understanding the cause of this, "that is, its analogy to the rest of the phenomena of the human mind," was similarly not part of his purpose (I, 26). His sole interest in honor as a motive was whether it was most often attached to social, semisocial, or antisocial intentions; this is what legislators must weigh in considering honor.[17] In contrast to a psychology whose object was to determine what we can know, Bentham insisted that he was only concerned with motives on account of the intentions they give birth to; he had no business with "purely speculative" motives that rest in the understanding (I, 46). In his opinion the first two books of Hume's *Treatise of Human Nature,* which dealt with precisely these questions for philosophy, might well be dispensed with (I, 268n.).

Despite his departure from the epistemological focus of most sensationalist psychology, Bentham absorbed its central idea and put it to use. No thought or action is disinterested. The natural history of these shows that each is the result of the operation of some motive (I, 212, 218). Self-interest does not characterize only one type of action called economic, but behavior in general. "The most exalted acts of virtue may be easily reduced to a calculation of good and evil," Bentham wrote, adding the caution that this is not to degrade or weaken them, but to "represent them as the effects of reason" (I, 13). Nothing he had learned from psychology led Bentham to accept absolute egoism, however, and he referred to the pleasures and pains of benevolence and malevolence in a nonegoistic sense in *An Introduction* (I, 18, 52-53, 69).[18] He carefully opposed a "levelling" view of self-interest, then, and used the term in a "large and extensive sense . . . comprehending all motives"; any other understanding of self-interest is ill-grounded in fact and pernicious in tendency (*OLG,* p. 70n.). Wherever his characterization of psychology was strictly egoistic, it took the form of a generalization: "In the general tenor of life, in every human breast, self-regarding interest is predominant" (IX, 5); and he put this generalization to use mainly in his work on constitutional law. If, in addition, he thought that legislators must make a broad assumption of egoism because they cannot know individuals, still egoism alone has nothing in particular to say about the content of legislation (IV, 52; X, 524).[19] Egoism is simply no adequate basis on which to predict behavior—it points, at most, to the continued existence of the species (IX, 5-6).

The chief use Bentham made of psychology can be briefly stated: he applied the teachings of historical psychology when his subject was the "force of law." Psychology gave scientific authority to his study of the operation of sanctions, a study inspired by his reading of Beccaria's work on punishment. Pleasure and pain are "efficient causes or means," Bentham had learned, and he defined sanctions as sources of motives (I, 14; *OLG,* p. 68). "The powers of nature may operate of themselves; but neither the magistrate, nor men at large *can* operate, nor is God in the case in question *supposed* to operate, but through the powers of nature" (I, 15). Political sanctions are the sources of motives of the legislator's own creation. The legislator must understand the force, or value, of sanctions, and in particular weigh his own against the action of rival or allied sanctions.[20] The point here is that pleasure and pain are not only, or in the first instance, the ends the legislator must have in view but also the instruments he has to work with. Sanctions supply motives for obedience, or means of social control, but they do not by themselves necessarily change men's interests. At the same time, psychology's teaching serves the legislator as a reminder that every law and its attendant sanction exposes some persons to suffering; it is a limiting idea (*OLG,* p. 54; I, 338, 398). Bentham intended psychology both to restrict the punitive actions of the legislator and to make them effective; his great value and aim was efficiency (I, 398).

The other consideration the legislator must take of pleasure and pain—happiness as the end of legislation—cannot be gotten from a historical study of motives alone. Knowledge of what men suffer from contributes to a rationalization of punishment and permits the classification of possible offenses. But a study of motives is not sufficient for deciding what the law ought to make an offense. As Bentham's discussion moved from sanctions and the force of law to the ends of legislation, his attention turned from a historical psychology of learning to social psychology.

Even where Bentham wrote about the operation of law, however, and drew lessons directly from historical psychology, his purposes led him to deal freely with questions that he knew psychology might treat with greater rigor. This is evident above all in *An Introduction,* where he discussed will and intention, and distinguished intention from motive. Psychology had taught Bentham to take care here, and he admitted that exciting causes and intentions are intimately connected and that he had been unable to keep them adequately distinct (I, 22n., 42). But distinct he meant them to be. *An Introduction* focused on penal law, and the result of Bentham's distinction between motive and intention was to allow for legal responsibility.[21] Intention is a composite idea, he explained. It encompasses both will and understanding, or consciousness (I, 35, 43), and "to the title of Consciousness belongs what is to be said of the goodness or badness of a man's intention, as resulting from the consequences of the act" (I, 43). Responsibility turns on neither the motives for an act nor the consequences of an act alone, then. Bentham was sensitive to the difficulty of designating where one act ends and another begins, of ascertaining whether an act is one act or several, and of distinguishing the part of the physical act that is willed from its innumerable consequences. These difficulties are precisely why his statement that intention comprises consciousness is so important (I, 35). Responsibility turns on an understanding of the circumstances of one's actions because consequences depend principally upon circumstances rather than motives (I, 43). Indeed, circumstances are misleadingly said to "attend" an act, Bentham cautioned, and this presents them as separate from and external to action. Instead, circumstances constitute an act and give it its character (*OLG,* p. 44). Bentham concluded: "An act which is unadvised with respect to any material circumstance is more or less culpable in proportion to the obligation which a man is under to inform himself of that circumstance."[22] According to this distinction between motive and intention, one need not desire the consequences of an act to be held responsible for it.[23] Bentham took a characteristically moderate position on legal responsibility, for the legal consequences of action are made to turn on neither purely subjective nor purely formal criteria. Clearly, intention is another thing entirely from Helvetius's "attention" and from Bentham's own description of motives as "interesting perceptions." The distinction between motive and intention, however problematic from the point of view of sensationalist psychology, was necessary for a theory of punishment, and points up the peculiarly legalistic view Bentham took of these subjects.

To read *An Introduction* is to comprehend that Bentham never deviated from the legalist's view that the crucial distinction between men is neither ruler and ruled nor independent and dependent, but criminal and innocent. In this distinction, more than anywhere else, security may be found, he thought—in the clarity of this divide. Psychology had adequately answered those "moralists" who would raise what they looked upon as weakness to the level of crime. Motives, psychology taught, are neutral (I, 60n.). Imputations about motives are out of order when it comes to responsibility not only because they cannot be known but also because they are irrelevant (II, 363, 415). On the other side, however, psychology threatened to transform crime into weakness. With "intention," Bentham affirmed his attachment to social consciousness, responsibility, and the requirements of legal order.

Helvetius was one of Bentham's closest ties with Lockean psychology, and it is in Helvetius's efforts and in the political import of his work that the points of Bentham's further departures from a psychology of learning are found. To repeat, Lockean psychology was concerned with the question "what can we know?" In the mental history of ideas, pleasure and pain are sovereign, but even though knowledge is limited to what sensations cause or occasion, this was no reason to feel constrained. For Locke himself, psychology was liberating; it assured that one's own reason is adequate for a life of happiness. Psychology was turned against dogma, but not against all principles and authorities, and Bentham recognized and applauded Locke's object—intellectual independence (X, 142).

Independence was the aspiration behind every psychology of learning, but Helvetius took a radical view of the matter. He was less concerned with what we can know than with why and what men have known. His interest was preeminently political: who determines the ideas men hold and who profits by what they know? For Helvetius, independence and dependence were matters of idea making, and power belonged to priests and legislators who invent and propagate our moral ideas. His was the first critical ideology: all ideas, and in particular standards, are disguises that can be stripped to reveal their egoistical origin.[24] Bentham had resort to this sort of unveiling himself, and *The Book of Fallacies* is not the only evidence that he took his master's work seriously and applied it when attacking authority. "Unhappily for the members of the democratical section [of the public]," Bentham wrote in his *Constitutional Code*, "their conceptions, their judgments, their suffrages, their language, have till this time been placed almost completely under the guidance, and almost, as it were, at the disposal of those of the aristocratical" (IX, 44).

Helvetius used psychology to explain the origin of ideas, but his analysis had nothing to say in defense of any of them. His object was to depreciate past moral ideas and authorities. Bentham recognized the forcefulness of psychology used in this way as a form of aggression, but he was not exclusively preoccupied with this sort of critical enterprise. And he distinguished between opinion (of which utility is admittedly one example) and fallacy, deception, or sophistry (II, 380). When Bentham made the security of men's expectations the end of utilitarian legislation, he revealed the distance between his political intentions and Helvetius's; Bentham took the lessons of psychology seriously and insisted that there is no escape from our opinions. Any attempt to disappoint or transform men's expectations can only produce misery. Besides, a psychology whose entire import is critical was inadequate for Bentham, since defense of some ideas was clearly part of his purpose. He was not content to "level" ideas to their egoistic causes. "There are two things," Bentham cautioned, "which are apt to be confounded, but which it imports us carefully to distinguish: the motive or cause, which, by operating on the mind of an individual, is productive of any act, and the ground or reason which warrants a legislator, or other bystander, in regarding that act with an eye of approbation" (I, 11). The principle of utility provides that reason. It may be unsusceptible of direct proof, for psychology had made a logical defense of ideas impossible. Utility, Bentham conceded, "may be taken for an act of mind; a sentiment" (I, 1n.). But utility as a rationale for law is and must be justifiable to the community (I, 2, 9).

It remains to say something more about the important differences of political purpose that separated Bentham from Helvetius. At the bottom of Helvetius's theory of knowledge and history lies a distinction between man's primitive mental organization and the other influences that cause his ideas; the latter, up to the present point in history at least, have been preponderant. For this distinction, Bentham was in Helvetius's debt, because it turned psychology away from attention to mental processes and toward social conditions. One part of *An Introduction* was particularly new and difficult, Bentham claimed, and that was the chapter outlining the circumstances that influence sensibility (I, 22n.). Given his preoccupation with legislation, Bentham focused on those circumstances the legislator can know—habitual occupation, pecuniary circumstances, and connections in the way of sympathy (I, 31). Comprehension of the social determinants of sensibility was important for Bentham's theory of punishment. And it was the basis of his discussion of injury; these are the points where individuals are disposed to suffer, he wrote, and all but one of Bentham's "natural" divisions of offenses rest on this classification (I, 137-139). Helvetius had pointed the way down this productive track.

However, the distinction between primitive organization and social influences also points to Bentham's divergence from Helvetius's work. Like all such distinctions, this one was intended to protect one part of the equation from the other, and Helvetius meant to defend man's physiological organization against the contamination of social influences. By their natural constitution men are equal, Helvetius thought, and it is political and moral ideas that distinguish and divide them. He insisted that these divisive ideas must be exposed and new ones propagated; he had limitless faith in education. Bentham rejected any view that attributed all to either nature or education. Both nature and education, he wrote, are the groundwork of supervening circumstances and are never in any case separately discernible (I, 27). He maintained this view consistently: disposition, for example, is "a kind of fictitious entity, feigned for the convenience of discourse, in order to express what there is supposed to be *permanent* in a man's frame of mind" (I, 60), and what is permanent there consists of both an original constitution and other influences on

38

sensibility. These can be neither discriminated nor radically transformed. Bentham's "natural" division of offenses includes those against property, reputation, and condition, as well as person (I, 99).

Bentham did not oppose Helvetius directly on this matter. He was simply more consistent than Helvetius. Helvetius believed that once the egoistical origin of moral and political ideas was revealed, men could be reeducated with ideas that conform to their equal mental constitutions; men could become similar and sympathetic. Helvetius transformed political problems into pedagogical ones.[25] His optimism was not unlike Hartley's, at least in its object and in its conviction of man's infinite perfectibility. Bentham shared the general hope for moral "discovery and improvement." But he rejected the distinctive aspiration of the Enlightenment by rejecting Helvetius's faith in intellectuals whose special interest in truth was supposed to mark them out as a new and peculiarly benevolent source of ideas (I, 227). Nothing Bentham had to say on the subject of education matched Helvetius's radical egalitarianism. No liberation from our social ego is possible, Bentham was certain.[26] Men can only move the earth if they first find another earth to stand on (I, 3), and nothing in Helvetius's psychology could account for this new leadership or its new morality. When he wrote that pleasure and pain are man's sovereign masters, Bentham wrote without Rousseau's sense of victimhood, but also without Helvetius's hope for equality. Besides, the political value underlying Helvetius's expectations was not one Bentham shared. He was skeptical whether even under the conditions of Panopticon Helvetius's educational schemes could produce the sort of equality he hoped for—uniformity (IV, 65). And in Bentham's view the aspiration itself smacked of arbitrariness and despotism. Uniformity is arbitrary because it is a state that offends common experience and understanding; it is despotic because diversity is the sole condition for general happiness. Utility is the rationale par excellence of morals and legislation where there is toleration of—even an invitation to—diversity. And toleration of diversity, Bentham knew, requires political authority and law, and with these, inequality (IX, 81).

Still, Bentham's general debt to Helvetius should not be obscured; he acknowledged it generously and often. It was Helvetius who turned psychology from its focus on learning to a study of power. Bentham followed him into the field of social psychology he had opened up. In doing so he entered a field that had been traversed earlier, and for many of the same purposes, by Hobbes.

Bentham's Social Psychology

Hobbes had accepted the rudimentary axioms of naturalism: "For Nature it selfe does often presse upon men those truths, which afterwards, when they look for somewhat beyond Nature, they stumble at". He meant by this the "truths" of appetite and aversion.[27] The *Leviathan* was perhaps both the first and the greatest modern invitation to introspection. Hobbes urged heart searching; Bentham, child of his time, mind searching, though when Bentham addressed legislators directly he too encouraged them to "study the human heart" (I, 35). In any case, what they sought was not the mental history of ideas but recognition for desires and their objects—what Bentham referred to in a refreshingly unscientific phrase as the *"unseemly parts"* of the mind (I, 219, 214; V, 598n.). Both discovered not pure egoism, and certainly not benevolence alone, but malevolence as well. Hobbes prefaced *Leviathan* with a warning that the objects of men's passions are easily kept from our knowledge; the character of men's hearts is "blotted and confounded" with "dissembling, lying, counterfeiting, and erroneous doctrines."[28] And Bentham echoed him: *"fig-leaves"* cover our unseemly parts (I, 218-219). Their exposure is likely to cause mortification; the more closely a man looks into the mechanism of his own mind, the more he will be repelled (II, 478).

Nonetheless, there is everything to be gained by this acquaintance, though psychology's usefulness for politics can come only where its revelations are confessed. Bentham went one step further with Hobbes when he elevated honesty to the position of chief, if not sole, virtue. He considered veracity so important that he added "offenses by falsehood" to his otherwise "natural" division of offenses, admitting that it was a "kind of botch" on his sensational system (I, 105, 98). For both Bentham and Hobbes, honesty consisted of acknowledging one's willfulness and in particular the "passion to be reckoned with," fear. Unveiling was first of all a matter of introspection, then, and not as in Helvetius's work a matter of attacking aggressors, but its purposes were no less purely political. Honesty was necessary in order to comprehend even the possibility of authority, Hobbes thought; introspection's findings inspire obedience. It was necessary for legal order and for utilitarian legislation especially, according to Bentham. He did not ask Hobbes's more profound question: "how is political society possible at all?" He never thought that given honesty order would necessarily follow, only that where there is no order honesty would lead men to substitute resistance for conspiracy and make the grounds of disagreement clear (IX, 37). Honesty is a condition of utilitarian legislation, because utility takes desires for its sole content. Finally, the administration of justice absolutely depends upon veracity (II, 210).

Together, introspection and the personal quality that must accompany it point to what Bentham shared with Hobbes and what distinguished their psychologies from the Lockean psychology of learning: their certainty that psychology has no political significance unless the desires uncovered by it are considered from the point of view of their consequences. They studied desires and their objects for their effects on other men's desires, and not their history. They shared an emphasis on will as self-preservation and on the sentiment by which the relation of one will to another is principally known, fear. And they recognized that from the standpoint of social psychology, fear and its positive counterpart, security, are inseparable from questions of equality.[29] Hobbes anticipated that men "in a quiet frame of mind" might acknowledge one another as equals, since each was able to kill the other. Indeed, this insight was the whole object of introspection. Bentham entertained these questions for the sake of legislation, and given his interest, fearfulness appeared as a token not so much of constitutional equality as of men's inequality. Men are not uniformly fearful; will, as Bentham understood it, aimed not only at avoiding death but also at the preservation of one's social self. It resisted any damage to *amour propre* and above all any disappointment of expectation (I, 54). Insecurity and inequality were as protean as society itself, and insecurity was precisely a measure of a man's social place. Although social psychology takes questions of security and equality to be inseparable in this way, still there is no doubt which of these took precedence. For Hobbes, the universality of fear and the concomitant desire for security were the cause of political order, but equality had nothing to say about the form authority should take. For Bentham, security of expectation was the chief end of law, and equality was a secondary concern.

Bentham used insecurity as Hobbes had used fear before him, then, without special reference to its objects, didactically, and to deliberate political purpose. If fear of death is the passion that inclines men to peace, then the state can be said to have a natural and universal basis.[30] If insecurity is the worst pain, as Bentham insisted, then the whole end of law is justified, for the care of security is the law's entire work and the law's alone (I, 307). In short, psychology established the basis for legalism as a value and for a legal system whose range extended as far and to as many objects as the sentiment of insecurity reached. The range of the legal system may be unlimited, but Bentham shared Hobbes's conviction that security itself is a limited end and is possible, and that by contrast equality is impossible in human affairs. At best, equality is a subsidiary value, and an instrumental one. The greatest social psychologist, Rousseau, took the opposite view, of course, and argued that where there is inequality security cannot exist, thus making equality the most important political concern. Bentham's social psychology denied Rousseau's claim; it was designed to point to security as the chief good. "Equality ought not to be favored, except in the cases in which it does not injure security," he wrote succinctly (I, 303). It is axiomatic that desire and disappointment are not equivalent pains; the principle of nondisappointment is the legislator's "chief and all-directing guide" (V, 266; III, 388-389), and the law considers equality with a view above all to equalizing losses (IX, 3; I, 306-307). Inequality may pose a threat to security, Bentham admitted, and that is why a degree of equality is necessary for legal order. But he considered that legalism had even fiercer enemies than the criminals who war on the rest for their livelihoods, and "anti-legal ideologies" is the theme of Chapter 3. Indeed, of these enemies, the fanatical desire for equality posed the greatest danger to security. Both Hobbes and Bentham used psychology, therefore, to combat views that denied security its central place in the "geneology of human feelings" and in political thought.

Both thinkers were aware that death was not always acknowledged as the worst evil or insecurity experienced as the worst pain. Introspection was prescribed as an antidote precisely where the evils of insecurity were not self-evident. Briefly, psychology was aimed against the worst threat to legal order—fanaticism, religious fanaticism in particular, but other visions as well. No one was more sensitive than Bentham to the fact that fanaticism denies all of the moderating ideas that accompany attention to fear. Because it envisions the possibility of a radical break between the present and the future, fanaticism allows men to risk or even court death. To the fanatic, the present is "but a point," Bentham wrote, and the fanatic looks to the future not for his own sake only, or even for the sake of the existing generation, but on behalf of the species (I, 360). He takes foresight to an extreme. Bentham's psychology sought to tame the future precisely by claiming that this sort of future-looking is unnatural and ultimately self-defeating. He emphasized as Hobbes had that death marks the end of the era within which men desire; desire is naturally limited to one's lifetime and to the goods that are part of men's common experience and expectation. He was never able to clarify at what point expectations become visionary, except to say that expectations are the result of social experience and correspond to common understanding. But even where fanatical visions are shared, and are not purely idiosyncratic, they are bound to be self-extinguishing, for they characteristically cramp the ordinary rewards of commerce (I, 5). Bentham called fanaticism "ascetic" because it pretends to allow men to escape the usual relationship between effort and reward. He concentrated on economic expectations for several reasons: they are measurable and comparable, they are common and antiaristocratic, and, as his psychology suggests, they are the chief defense against fanaticism. There is no better argument against the attractions of fanatical aspirations—especially the revolutionary goal of equality—than the prediction that if realized, these goals would wreck commercial society.

The point here is that naturalist psychology serves as a basis for legal order in Bentham's thought by reducing the future to the range of ordinary expectations. The end of law, he repeated, is security of expectation, and Bentham was always cautious about promising that the principle of utility would institute "positive good" (I, 102n.; I, 304, 318). The immediate descendant of the principle of utility is the principle of non-disappointment. It is entirely conservative, and points up the special nature of Bentham's radicalism. Utility is mainly negative; it opposes fanaticism, "continual fresh divisions of the earth." And it opposes custom, resistance to all change. But based as it is on naturalism, utility will oppose custom only where established expectations are frustrated by it. From the point of view of utility, then, discrepancies between expectation and custom (specifically the common law) are simply a matter of circumstance. They are not, like expectation and fanaticism, essentially diverse, because custom need not be antilegalistic. Nonetheless, Bentham's purpose in distinguishing expectation and custom is clear and not at all trivial. Utility looks at the expectations of individuals and not at custom, or general opinion, or rules, and it thereby allows for reform. Of course, the moderating import of a psychology that emphasizes security is liable to abuse. If security of expectation were to replace custom as a rationale for law, expectation might become the psychological equivalent of appeals to ancestry or ancient usage, which appear conservative but are used to perpetuate and even extend political aggression in practice. Any aspiration might be expressed conservatively as if it were merely an effort to secure some men against the possibility of disappointment. The terms "economy" and "frugality," Bentham observed, were used to indicate preservation only, but acquisition entered "by *stealth*" (I, 214). This abuse is unavoidable, he knew. What matters most of all is that political aggression neither employ the rhetorical language nor admit the revolutionary aspirations of fanaticism, which makes any legal order inconceivable.

Reacting against what he viewed as one threat to legal order, Bentham sought to tame the future by retrieving it from ascetic visions, and to claim the future for utility: what is uncontrollable with respect to time is uncontrollable with respect to anything else (*TL*, p. 201). Asceticism's danger is that it reduces the present to a point, but "caprice" poses a different threat to legal order and Bentham used psychology to underscore its dangerousness as well. Caprice is shear spontaneity; it makes the present everything. Legislation is equally in need of protection against this psychological deviation, which he called aestheticism. It is this purpose that lends importance to Bentham's simple statement—which he believed derived plainly from psychology—that happiness is pleasure and security (I, 14). With security he introduced into the idea of happiness the very thing that pleasure itself does not necessarily imply: future time, foresight, or expectation. Security, Bentham wrote, "necessarily embraces the future" (*TL*, pp. 96-97). Hobbes had similarly made future time critical by emphasizing that the power that men ceaselessly pursue is the present means to future good; self-preservation, he had insisted further, requires anticipation.[31] Where fear and insecurity are the worst evils, future time is bound to be at the center of psychology—albeit carefully delimited to life on earth and to the range of ordinary expectations.

For Bentham, the disposition to look forward is natural to men. Pleasure and pain by anticipation are easily recognizable and are precisely what distinguish them from brutes (I, 308). In all of his legal writings, he advised the legislator that alarm is evil as well as pain; in many cases, the only thing that can justify the rigor of the law is the fear some offense arouses (I, 77; *TL*, p. 247). As a psychological phenomenon, expectation is a commonplace, Bentham thought: foresight is no feat. It is not in any case something that he felt compelled to explain, and Bentham's distance from the concerns of Lockean psychology is once again apparent.

Locke's *Essay* had shown that the statement "happiness is pleasure and security" is a profound one. The two goods stand in uneasy relation to each other; from the point of view of Locke's psychology, they seem at first to conflict, and their joint tenure in the field of happiness is the great accomplishment of the mind. It will be recalled that pleasure and pain are movements toward and away from continual states of uneasiness, and that Locke's object was to explain how men escape this tyranny of sensation. His solution entailed a distinction between short-term and long-term interest, or pleasure and happiness, which includes foresight and security. But the solution is not a simple one; all of the apparatus of the mind is required to reconcile pleasure and security. Indeed, it demands the "candle of the Lord."

Where happiness comprises security, property is sure to be its most common object. The feat of transforming pleasure into happiness is illustrated in Locke's *Second Treatise on Government,* where he considers the change from possession sufficient to meet immediate needs to estate and its security. The key is the invention of money; the world was given by God to the industrious and the rational; accumulation and abundance are signals of rationality, and constitute man's keenest enjoyment as well. Bentham did not disagree, but he refused abundance the status of a triumph for the morally and intellectually strong (I, 309).

Bentham must have been sensitive to the delicacy of the equilibrium between pleasure and foresight since aestheticism and asceticism are precisely these two taken to extremes. Where civil law was concerned, however, he simply asserted that foresight is a universal and constant experience. Sometimes he even characterized pleasure as the enjoyment of an expectation, and property as established expectation; property, in this view, is altogether a creature of the mind (I, 19, 308). He can be forgiven simplifying in this way, because his concern was not to explain expectation as a psychological phenomenon but to defend the view that where there is law, security of expectation and not pleasure alone must be its rationale. But his difference with Locke becomes important as the argument proceeds.

What for Locke was a quiet triumph was for Bentham a commonplace. It is in the nature of want itself, he claimed, to produce both labor and foresight (I, 303). Subsistence naturally leads to abundance, which is "produced by degrees, by the continued operation of the same causes which had provided for subsistence: there is no opposition between these two objects" (I, 304; IX, 1). The most profound thinker of all on this subject agreed with Bentham that foresight, property, and abundance are one; but Rousseau insisted thay they are all terrible and unnatural and need to be accounted for, because they all result in misery. Bentham went one great step toward concurring with Rousseau's view when he admitted that aversion to labor is axiomatic (I, 307; VIII, 598). But he proceeded to reject Rousseau's insights and to do so without any defense of his own. He had an excuse for ignoring the subtleties of Locke's psychology —their interests were diverse—but Bentham had no excuse for passing by the insights Rousseau offered, and this he did. Subsistence and security are both "like life itself" (I, 303), Bentham asserted, and abundance is their "inevitable tree." If labor is painful, still even the savage labors. Before there is law, want—armed with every pain—had commanded labor, sharpened courage, inspired foresight, and developed all of the faculties of man; the only difference between civilized man and the savage is that the latter's work is "fruitful in calamity" (I, 307). And what is more, desires extend only with the power of gratifying them (I, 304; IX, 7). Men are not tormented by impossibilities. There is no such thing as luxury, or superfluity, because no one can have more than he wants (Stark, I, 113). Moderation, as Bentham presented it, is neither the work of reason nor even the result of skepticism but the ordinary course of want itself. He ignored the noble psychological settlement that gave such satisfaction to Locke, and he simply denied the misery that haunted Rousseau. He claimed for his psychology a piece of both their worlds: labor and foresight were as painful as they were for Rousseau and as natural as they were for Locke.

Bentham was not adding anything new to political thought when he stated that the law transforms possession into property—that, it was generally agreed, was the great object of political society. But he was careful to deny that this was in any way a profound change, and no contract (and most often no state of nature) marked the transition in his work. For the law adds nothing to man that was not there before. If "law alone has accomplished what all the natural feelings were not able to do," it is not because Bentham took an educational view of law; the law does not create new desires. It merely encourages labor and foresight, which are the creatures of want itself (I, 307). A "strong and permanent expectation results from law alone: that which was only a thread in a state of nature, becomes a cable, so to speak, in a state of society" (I, 309).

Security of expectation arises first of all, then, in connection with property, and its protection is the work of the law. Ordinarily, Bentham objected to appeals to the state of nature. He used the image in this brief account of property, though, an account calculated to emphasize the pain of loss, rather than the pain of privation, and to stress nondisappointment as the law's chief object. Still, the relation between property and privation was clear to Bentham. Discussions about property were, he knew, inseparable from social psychology—that is, from the bearing one man's happiness has on others. For social psychology, the problem of general happiness is not conceived as a problem of autonomous men desiring the same scarce thing. Social psychology recognizes instead that some men's desires actually determine the desires of other men, and provide them with their content. Social psychology is an analysis of dependence. The idea makes its appearance in Bentham's work with his notion of "service" and his characterization of all social relations as mutual services (*TL,* pp. 197, 187; I, 470; *OLG,* pp. 57-58, 60). The universal existence of services was, in Bentham's view, self-evident, and he did not offer an account of the origins of dependence and social subordination. Services, like power in Hobbes's theory, come in an infinite variety and are as protean as happiness itself (IX, 12). It is services that the law formalizes into rights and obligations (III, 179-180) and there is no better evidence of the range, indeed the illimitable range, of the legal system in Bentham's thought than its basis in the idea of securing services, and not property alone. At the same time, however, what distinguishes Bentham's social psychology from others and especially Rousseau's is his emphasis on relations that are typically economic. When he attacked aristocratic rule or the legal profession, Bentham did attend to the diverse forms and instruments of dependence and subjugation, and some of these instruments are discussed in Chapters 3 and 6. Where his subject was civil law, however, Bentham always had in view the fanatical disposition for equality, which is security's chief threat. In countering this disposition, he treated problems of property and poverty as just that—"problems"—without apportioning blame. In his work on economics and civil law, he spoke of even the most unequal economic relations as if they were unoppressive. In short, he discussed property and privation as nearly as possible apart from class analysis.

Rousseau wrote about property quite differently. All of the gains of abundance are only for the few, he insisted, and more important, all riches depend upon and are even caused by someone else's poverty. According to his social psychology, every pleasure is at the expense of someone else's pain. Rousseau's was an excruciating vision of universal misery and its inexorable course. Bentham ignored it in his work on property. He denied that anyone was responsible for relations of unequal economic dependence, and he did not adopt a psychology that made the worst pains of dependence inevitable. Riches are indeed relative to poverty, he admitted, but riches are not dependent upon poverty, nor do they cause it. Poverty is simply the primitive condition of the human race (I, 309). Although all pains are privations, what one does not have is not necessarily a privation (I, 19).[32] "If this were not the case, every man would experience this evil with regard to every thing which he did not obtain, and the causes of evil being infinite, every one ought to find himself infinitely miserable" (I, 307). (And so Rousseau had found men.) Bentham went on: neither is it poverty that causes abundance. Abundance is the work of the laws: "Without law there is no security; and, consequently no abundance, and not even a certainty of subsistence" (*TL*, p. 109). He rejected unhesitatingly Beccaria's suggestion that the right of property is a "terrible right and may not perhaps be necessary" (I, 309).

According to Bentham's "mental pathology," it is necessary and it is not terrible. For in creating property, the laws have been benefactors to those who remain in their original poverty; they participate more or less in the advantages of civilized society (I, 309). This is so, Bentham thought, chiefly because abundance is the surest guarantee of universal subsistence (I, 360, 309). In an "infinitely complicated" system of economic relations, the subsistence of most men derives from the wealth of one part (I, 311). The poor profit indirectly from security of property as well. The laws that provide for the disposition of wealth by means of wills, for example, protect parents against the ingratitude of their children. These laws affect manners generally, and even those with nothing to leave profit by them (I, 337). Bentham could write, with Locke, that individual interests are the only real interests, without admitting the pains that this created for Rousseau, because he was certain that by defending individual interests men in general would be protected. Abundance is produced by the same causes that produce subsistence, and "those who have condemned abundance, under the name of luxury, have never understood this connection" (I, 304). Without security and the abundance it permits, the only equality possible is an "equality of misery" (I, 307).

It is not that the law has nothing to do with equality. Clearly, the law does more than nature, for the principle of utility prescribes an assurance of subsistence for everyone. Bentham did not make too much of this distinction, however. He insisted here, just as he had when he wrote about the creation of laws to secure property, on the continuity between nature and the state. The advantages of legally secured subsistence were plain enough, but for Bentham legalism was a matter of degree and of the political values served by the law, and not an absolute condition. Thus, he pointed to continuity between nature and the state by observing that the claim for subsistence was not unconditional, since it was possible that even in civilized society famine or economic stagnation would argue against providing universal subsistence (II, 534). He also pointed to continuity by insisting that the indigent labor in return for relief (VIII, 401). On the other hand, Bentham was careful to explain that universal subsistence was indeed the work of the law. The principle of utility recommends direct state action or state licensing to ensure subsistence, and if this recommendation is contingent like every other, it does not wait on or draw its character from the actions of institutions other than the state. Bentham did not claim that by making provision for the poor the state substitutes for the family. He did not intend public assistance to replace voluntary benevolence.[33] He described laws that supply subsistence as rationalizations of charity,[34] but sympathy is not their rationale (I, 315-316). Utility alone prescribes universal subsistence: simply, the worst misery is death. Utility thus makes a distinction between indigence, which is lack of subsistence, and poverty, which is always relative to abundance (III, 228; I, 316); for the misery of utter indigence certainly outweighs the disappointment that may result from forced "contributions" (I, 316). Bentham's mental pathology suggests axioms for assessing contributions (I, 304-307), though most often his discussions of taxation occur quite apart from any direct consideration of redistribution. But he admitted the limitations of these axioms; even if they were better than any other estimate legislators might use, still, he cautioned, no adequate treatise existed on the manner of assessing either contributions or distributions for the relief of indigence (TL, p. 133). Bentham warned too about propagating a "right to subsistence" unaccompanied by specifications as to its cost and the administrative organization and procedures required to put it into effect (II, 534). Supervision was one of his characteristic concerns, and Bentham's own scheme for pauper relief was more than anything else a treatise on management.

Bentham's thoughts on subsistence point to two things above all. They indicate his interest in the range of state activity, its unified character, and the details of its administration. Of more immediate concern here is the fact that Bentham's argument for providing subsistence and apportioning its cost sets aside all questions of the responsibility for indigence. Bentham made every effort to deny poverty the appearance of a wrong done by one class to another. In his pamphlets on paper money and inflation, for example, he relieves country bankers of blame, even though it was their issuances that caused prices to rise and exasperated the misery of the poor (Stark, II, 434-435; Stark, III, 409-410). And he denied that the responsibility for indigence lies with the poor. Indigence, he wrote, comes in all shapes and from all causes, and the great mass of men is always liable to slip into poverty—above all because their livelihood depends upon their labor. Accidents, the "revolutions of commerce" (including economic stagnation), natural calamities, disease, and age, and not laziness or prodigality alone, are among the causes of indigence (I, 314). The law may provide for subsistence, and this would be only "to a certain extent" a law against industry. Even the best legal system cannot prevent "inevitable reverses," and experience proves "the vanity of human prudence" (I, 314-315).[35] It is just not true that the punishment of poverty falls only on the guilty (I, 314; *TL,* p. 133). Bentham's language seems to relieve poverty of the status of a crime.[36] It follows that the law must not only provide subsistence but also equalize the losses that result from reverses and calamities. Minimizing disappointment is, after all, its chief business, and Bentham shared his contemporaries' interest in insurance and indemnification schemes that, in his work, amount to social security (VIII, 410-413; I, 306-307). The law has this to do with equality, then: it protects equality where it exists, and provides equality of subsistence where it does not exist.

Of special note in all this is the range of the legal system where utility is its rationale. The distinction utility makes between subsistence and poverty served to guarantee subsistence and to oppose the aspiration to absolute equality. It was not meant as a general prohibition against legal measures to ensure economic production or to relieve poverty, and Bentham was certainly not oblivious to the miseries of poverty. The state does more than provide subsistence; it recognizes poverty as the great social problem of modern times. The state should be organized to seek the causes of poverty and to effect precautions and relief, Bentham thought. The principle of utility prescribes state activity, and the state's "statistic function" alone is an active business. Bentham recommended measures to deal with famine (stockpiles and price-fixing), unemployment, and the rise of prices, among others. The merits of these recommendations are of no concern here; the point is that the range of the legal system and the institutions that support it are evident in Bentham's economic writings. Briefly, the state is designed to act, not to do nothing.[37]

Why does utility take an interest in equality beyond ensuring subsistence? Bentham makes two arguments that appear side by side, and with varying emphasis, in his writings on economics and civil law. For one thing, subsistence itself demands concern for equality. The distribution of wealth most favorable to universal subsistence, he observed, is one where degrees between the most and least rich are "regular and insensible" (Stark, I, 116). One of the purposes of his annuity scheme was to have the state encourage the poor to save with interest, and if Bentham spoke of frugality as a matter of virtue, it was in his mind a matter of inequality as well (Stark, II, 295n.; I, 314). Given the indissoluble connection between subsistence and abundance, it may be the business of law to promote equality or not, depending on what action is most likely to result in conditions necessary for production. Whether or not the state acts or licenses action, whether it supports or discourages monopoly, for example, are altogether contingent questions that turn on the circumstances necessary for abundance, and Bentham gave particular attention to the needs of developing industries, as *Defense of Usury* reveals (Stark, I, 121; Stark, III, 52).[38] In every instance, the state's economic actions, like all its other actions, are measured by their efficiency. Most often necessity demands no more of the state than removing the bars to economic development, Bentham thought. It is, though, the work of the law to create the conditions for abundance, and clearly readers have found it difficult to make the case that Bentham was doctrinaire on the subject of state intervention.[39]

Bentham's other explanation for utility's concern with equality is different. It states that inequality must be reduced in order to combat fanaticism. Security increases with opulence, Bentham thought, and inequality is the inescapable accompaniment of opulence, but security does not increase proportionately with inequality (Stark, III, 327). There is a class of men, Bentham wrote, that wages war on the rest for its subsistence (Stark I, 110-111). This fact calls for more than just providing universal subsistence, and one argument for Bentham's annuity scheme and for issuing small shares in his joint-stock National Charity Company was that these would give the "little monied interest" a "palpable interest in the support of . . . government" (Stark, II, 205, 57, 296-298; III, 145; VII, 370n.). The relationship between security and equality is a precarious one, clearly, and the primacy of security is apparent. Inequality must not be reduced by disturbing property. Bentham would maintain the existing distribution everywhere, and he knew exactly how diverse and unequal these distributions were. Still: "When security and equality are in opposition, there should be no hesitation; equality should give way . . . The establishment of equality is a chimera: the only thing which can be done is to diminish inequality" (I, 311). A single error in attempts to produce equality "may overturn the whole social order" (I, 302). The disruption would be fatal, because insecurity paralyzes men and causes them to stop investing their productive capital (I, 310). More important, it would be fatal because of the disposition that currently makes equality itself a goal. Some diminishing of inequality may be necessary to prevent disorder, Bentham thought, but the demand for equality is precisely the form fanaticism takes in contemporary politics.

The disposition that inclines to equality argues, more strongly than anything else, for security before equality as the end legislators must have in view. This disposition is fanatical; it imparts to every effort to achieve equality a character entirely different from that of policies to relieve indigence or other concrete miseries. These policies are always remediable. But the desire for equality is inspired by envy and indignation at wealth; it is fundamentally a desire for revenge, which is insatiable and incorrigible. Thus, the instruments necessary to attain equality do not admit of moderate application or of degrees (I, 362; IX, 14). The "utmost conceivable equality" belongs only to the realm of physics, Bentham warned. Among men, the utmost conceivable equality is identity or uniformity, and it will always be imperfect. Especially where property is concerned, equality would necessitate "continual fresh divisions of the earth" and result in perpetual revolution. Equality is opposed to productive activity, indeed to all legal order, and the aspiration for equality would destroy commercial society. The desire for equality signals a return to savagery, in Bentham's mind, and he quoted: *"Devant eux des citiés, derrière eux des déserts"* (I, 312). As he understood it, the longing for equality is therefore different even from the criminal's simple aversion to labor. It is self-defeating, for where abundance is impossible there can be only misery. And it is pure aggression. It is the one illustration in Bentham's writing of Rousseau's fearful psychological symmetry, according to which one man's pain causes, indeed constitutes, another man's pleasure. The desire for equality, Bentham wrote, is a taste for blood (I, 321).

If, despite this, Bentham once remarked that security and equality might be reconciled, this reconciliation was not a moral one: the legislator is not an educator at whose hands subjects are remade. A law is not a precept (*OLG*, p. 11). The legislator does not, therefore, teach all men to love equality so that it can be instituted without disruption. "The legislator is not the master of the dispositions of the human heart: he is only their interpreter and their servant. The goodness of his laws depends upon their conformity to the general *expectation*" (I, 322). And, Bentham recognized, these expectations bring with them inequality. Faced with this admission, Rousseau designed utopias to make the costs to men clear; Bentham simply offered his proposal "Supply Without Burden," a plan for diminishing inequality by a severe tax on certain inheritances. In fact, his escheat proposal was less a resolution of the conflict between security and equality than an acknowledgment of the limits of mediating between the two. According to mental pathology, a law to diminish inequality must "await the natural epoch which puts an end to hopes and fears, the epoch of death" (I, 321; *TL,* p. 122). Escheat alone allows equality to join abundance in forming the "inevitable tree" of security and subsistence. Their reconciliation was in no way moral; it was not even immediately practicable (Stark, I, 287). But it was psychologically possible, and Bentham gave this possibility its due.

Security was the law's principal object, and in Bentham's mind it took precedence not only over equality but over other goals as well. He recommended more than once that new laws of his own design be enacted but that their commencement be deferred "to a distant period" (I, 291n.; Stark, I, 287). His *Constitutional Code* was so novel, for example, that its very publication might retard the institution of republican government, and he did not expect to live to see his proposals instituted. Bentham appeared not to regret the slow pace of reform in this case; he would not want to claim for his work any result which was not unsullied by "admixture with evil in those shapes which are inseparable from all change, preceded by hostile contention, or sudden and uncompensated transfer of property or power" (IX, 2). Since on one matter above all Bentham was insistent, that no act of government is pure good, his patient disclaimer reflects his view that of the two pains of privation—desire and disappointment—the latter is worse. Happily for the legislator, the choice of evils is fixed by the "genealogy of human feeling."

Utility's scientific character comes not so much from its claim to precision as from its basis in naturalism (I, 16). Even if the axioms of mental pathology are correct and the legislator's calculations are exact, utility is not a sure instrument of prediction. It looks to the consequences of law and is therefore a better rationale for legislation than any other, but utility's prescriptions rest on nothing more certain than "the probability of certain future contingencies" (I, 291; *OLG,* p. 37). The legislator, Bentham advised, can make only a "rough and almost random guess . . . by analogy" of a law's effect in securing expectations or introducing some new "positive good" (II, 402). The character of any law utility recommends is therefore experimental (III, 321) and subject to revocation or change. Bentham had a most expressive phrase for utilitarian legislation, caught as it was between custom and policy: "defeasible perpetuity" (*OLG,* p. 75).[40] He was entirely consistent and insightful when he called constitutionalism "the most interesting of all temporal subjects" (IX, 2), for constitutionalism is an attempt not to restrain rulers simply, but to combine the advantages of perpetuity with those of corrigibility.

"Expectation" is Bentham's middle ground between custom and "continual fresh divisions of the earth." It can be said for Bentham that when he had the principle of utility secure expectations before anything else, he understood the range of the legal system this permitted and at the same time recognized the limits of what he recommended. He advised security first without any suggestion that the origin of established expectations or the consequence of securing them had anything to do with reason or virtue. The claim for making expectations the basis of law was purely and properly legalistic: men are enabled to form a general plan of conduct.

3. Antilegal Ideologies

> According to this principle [utility], to legislate is an affair of observation and calculation; according to the ascetics, it is an affair of fanaticism; according to the principle of sympathy and antipathy, it is a matter of humour, of imagination, of taste. (*TL,* 10)

Bentham presented the principle of utility as a rationale for legislation. Because utility pays attention to the expectations of individuals, he claimed, it offers the best chance for legal security and for a regular course of conduct in the modern state. No matter how extravagant his personal ambitions sometimes appeared, and no matter how often his discussions of utility were imbued with truly radical optimism, still, no one understood better than he the special limits of that principle. Legal order is only possible where political consensus for utility's accommodations exists, he knew, and Bentham had little to say about the conditions of consensus. He did not promise that utility could create these conditions or produce agreement about laws. He was certain only that legislation provides effective security where the consensus it rests on is neither dictated nor assumed, but arrived at before men's eyes. It must be clear, in other words, that the laws owe their existence, their fairness, and the agreement they enjoy to the political efforts of identifiable men to take account of diverse and changing desires. Utility provides this clarity. It appeals to the public judgment and invites its concurrence in legislation; utility encourages obedience (I, 161).

Utility does not ensure agreement about laws, then. It does set out the grounds on which men could agree or disagree (I, 287, 291; II, 495). Utility gives to every discussion respecting laws a clear and determinate point of view; it puts every political question upon "an issue of fact" (II, 495;

III, 286).[1] In short, utility is the rationale that confronts political questions directly. Personalities, antiquity, the law of nature, the law of nations, and a thousand other terms have been invented to prevent recourse to this direct method, Bentham wrote (I, 161). Utility may not produce consensus, but it is certain to "disarm all cheats and fanatics" (I, 161). Bentham left no doubt that the chief claim for utility is mainly negative; it exposes subjectivity and fanaticism in political affairs. It is antirhetorical.

Other so-called principles of legislation (Bentham had in mind higher-law standards) are, by contrast, rhetorical. They are vague and often empty of content. He did not deny that in the past natural rights, for example,[2] had effected certain useful work and liberal improvements in political affairs; still, he never retreated from the position that appeals to natural rights signify a "penury of argument," and that they are prejudicial to the true science of legislation (II, 524).[3] Bentham's main concern with natural rights was neither historical nor logical, however, but overwhelmingly contemporary and political. The idea of legislation can now be understood: men make laws in response to immediately felt evils. In practice, therefore, assent to formulae like natural rights is really at the same time assent to quite specific measures (I, 303; II, 493-494, 503). And advancing particular measures by pointing to their correspondence with a formula is a dangerous political device—dangerous and more disturbing than the phrase "impropriety of language" first suggests. For when the standards used to promote legislation are rhetorical, they serve as cloaks for despotism. Natural rights "hold out a mask for every crime; —they are every villain's armoury—every spendthrift's treasury" (II, 524).

It is useful in this connection to recall that Bentham was the self-proclaimed disciple of the master of eighteenth-century ideological unveiling. Helvetius reserved his fiercest attacks for the clergy, who exercised power in a special way—by means of erudition. Ideas, Bentham learned, are a successful form of aggression. He duplicated Helvetius's efforts in his own detailed accounts of the self-serving language and rituals of the legal profession. He also provided a classification of the motives and styles of political conservatism in *The Book of Fallacies*. When it came to higher-law notions, though, Bentham was not content to disclose the motives that encourage this sort of fallacious reasoning; he was less concerned to reveal the specific self-interest behind each appeal to higher law than he was to point out the disposition common to men who brandish these formulae.[4] Bentham called this disposition despotic. This chapter reviews his discussion of the despotic disposition and its several ideological expressions.

One theme unites Bentham's several attacks on higher law: subscribers to natural rights and every other higher-law standard are not satisfied with the sort of consensus at which utility aims. They demand unanimity in political affairs (I, 9n.). The American Declaration of Independence, he wrote, was the product of enthusiasm; it was promulgated by men who were "unanimous and hearty" about the measures they had agreed upon (I, 154). The desire to establish fundamental laws is an "old conceit," Bentham acknowledged, and he was not without sympathy for the longing for universal agreement (II, 494). But want is not supply, hunger is not bread, and reasons for wishing there were such a thing as natural rights are not rights (II, 501). When he criticized higher-law standards for confusing "is" and "ought," he did not want to see moral judgments put aside when the merits of a law are considered. After all, utility too aims at the coincidence between moral principle and law. He criticized higher-law standards instead for insisting that where the correspondence between moral principle and law is wanting, the law is not just a bad one, it is no law at all and is void. This is deliberate obfuscation, Bentham argued; it is cheating men for their own good (I, 269). And no good can come of it. For if attempts at dictating unanimity do not produce irrational acquiescence, they produce equally irrational denial (II, 495, 500, 524). The French Revolution may well have "meant opportunity above all," for Bentham.[5] It meant an audience for particular projects, and an opportunity to turn his attention to representation and other questions of constitutional law.[6] Most important, the revolution provided an occasion to demonstrate that natural rights are "words that speak daggers"; the revolution "displayed their import by a practical comment" (II, 500, 524). And this import was not restricted to the formulae of revolutionary democracy. All higher-law standards are similarly evidence of political enthusiasm and of the desire for unanimity. They all constitute "fighting words."

Only utility assumes and accepts the heterogeneity that characterized Bentham's "busy age" (I, 227), where men have their differences about matters of judgment and taste, science and art, the ordinary occurrences of life, "in short, about everything which has a name" (II, 265-266). Utility seeks agreement with this diversity as an acknowledged starting point; it takes into account the different kinds and degrees of human sensibility. Only utility actually does what one rhetorical formula—"common sense"—pretends to do, Bentham wrote: it shares power (I, 8n.).

Utility, in a word, is conciliatory. In Bentham's hands, it is best understood, even solely understood, as a reaction against every enthusiastic disposition and political formula that is not similarly conciliatory.

Bentham claimed that the principle of utility afforded the best chance for legal security. And he applauded it for presenting politics with a new and humane value—efficiency. It cannot be emphasized enough, however, that neither security nor efficiency is possible or of special worth without toleration. Toleration may be the personal quality belonging to those who employ the principle of utility; it is assuredly the consequence of utility in practice. But whether toleration is a disposition or the condition utility produces, the relation between toleration and utility in Bentham's mind is clear. It can be seen, for example, with regard to the critical matter of truthfulness. Honesty and publicity play a central part in Bentham's political thought. Truthfulness is "one of the elements of our existence," "necessary as the light of day to us" (I, 78); all human society depends upon truthfulness, Bentham wrote, for every one of our judgments relies on the observations of others (I, 78). Honesty is necessary if legal order is to prevail in the modern state, because utility takes desires for its content and because the evidence necessary for the administration of justice absolutely depends upon it. Even so, Bentham was emphatic: truthfulness should not be encouraged where the public mind is "infected with the disease of intolerance" (IX, 53). His principal argument against sectarianism is that religious disputes encourage men to make false declarations and allow some men privileged lies (I, 565). And intolerance only begins with religion; it extends to all questions of politics and taste, to every idiosyncrasy (IX, 53).[7] Persecution need not be violent to be effective, Bentham knew; "secret persecutions" occur in most places; civil punishments, political incapacities, and threatening laws create "a humiliating situation for classes of men who owe their tranquility only to a tacit indulgence, a continual pardon" (I, 565). Toleration truly exists only where it does not go by that haughty name, and utility is the principle that makes consideration of every desire a commonplace. In short, utility is a consistent rationale for law precisely because no preference is excluded from its view; utility places no value on unanimity. It is not rhetorical; it is not despotic.

Bentham introduced aestheticism and asceticism as the two principles adverse to utility in Chapter 2 of *An Introduction*. If he were giving an exhaustive account of moral principles or presenting categories for analyzing moral principles, his discussion there would be entirely inadequate. As it is, Bentham explained that he would not address the critical questions of moral philosophy at all; he chose not to consider how men derive notions of right or what notions of right they can persist in consistently. He took as his subject the narrower question: How can men justify their moral sentiments to the community (I, 9n.)? He argued that utility is the only consistent rationale for law, the only rationale employable by any form of government determined to be a good one and acceptant of the inescapability of diversity. It turns out that aestheticism and asceticism are not exactly principles adverse to utility at all: aestheticism is not a principle, and asceticism is utility "misapplied." For Bentham, they represent the most common forms the despotic disposition takes in its insistence upon unanimity, and the mark of both aestheticism and asceticism is intolerance. They both find expression in current ideologies, and are subscribed to by specific social classes.

Aestheticism and asceticism lie behind what Bentham conceived of as the two contemporary antilegal ideologies. Asceticism characterizes revolutionary fanatics, whose favorite political formula is natural rights; aestheticism characterizes the aristocracy and its allies, who are moved by antipathy to reform and whose political formulae are taken from classical rhetoric. Bentham was perhaps the first to treat these ideologies together and to suggest what it is the two share. His observations would become familiar later, when these dispositions made themselves manifest in the extremes of anarchy and reaction. Both asceticism and aestheticism are deliberate flights from utility, he argued; they are antilegal and antimodern; and they may be adopted alternately by the same men.[8]

The principle of asceticism seems to be absolutely opposed to utility. It approves or disapproves of actions insofar as they tend to diminish happiness, and the purest example of asceticism is the monk who administers self-torments. If ascetics do not always court pain in this fashion, they do renounce ordinary pleasures and happiness as it is commonly understood. Originally, asceticism was a philosophic stance, Bentham recognized; "certain hasty speculators" observed that incommensurate evils resulted from the enjoyment of some pleasures, and in an effort to avoid these effects, they rejected ordinary pleasures entirely (I, 6). Philosophic asceticism is aptly described, therefore, as utility "misapplied." A second feature of philosophic asceticism separates it further from utility, he added. The ascetic typically adopts a moralistic stance. Not content to abstain from common pleasures, he rejects them as vulgar and gross. He proclaims himself indifferent to the pains suffered by ordinary men. Or, in another attempt to distinguish himself, he erects his own hierarchy of pleasures, which he designates "the *honestum*" or "the *decorum,*" in order to cleanse them "from the sordes of its impure original" (I, 5). The attitude philosophic ascetics share, Bentham claimed, is pride. And pride is expressed in the ascetic's self-conscious and doctrinaire flight from utility.

Asceticism is encountered less often in the form of a speculative doctrine, however, than it is as a rejection of the common pursuit of happiness in practice. The usual motive for the familiar forms of asceticism is fear. The threat of divine punishment, for example, prevents religious ascetics from participating in the enjoyments that engage other men (I, 4). Bentham was sufficiently a child of the Enlightenment that he explained what he called the superstitious fear of a splenetic deity by ignorance. In fact, he took an inclusive view of the relation between ignorance and fear, and used asceticism to describe the disposition that comes from not knowing the consequences of action in general. Renunciations of pleasure need not be religious, then. Men also cease pursuing pleasures when they are uncertain whether ordinary labor will result in ordinary rewards; insecurity of property always results in torpor and lack of effort, he observed. Asceticism is the disposition shared by those to whom the ways of God or of action in the world are simply incomprehensible. Where arbitrariness seems to govern every available course of conduct, fear prevails and paralysis is certain to follow. Asceticism accompanies an abject condition in life. Ignorance is remediable, and even the causes of economic insecurity may be known and guarded against. But not all asceticism can be overcome by the good laws, security, and common sense that utility brings, Bentham cautioned. Revolutionary fanaticism too is an ascetic flight from contemporary values, but the motive that inspires it prevents its being easily brought back to mundane calculations.

If in the past asceticism has been marked by fearfulness or pride, in its latest and most virulent form asceticism is inspired by pride's other side—envy. The contemporary expression of the repudiation of common pleasures is the "right to equality," Bentham argued. Envy moves men to claim this right, and the aspiration to equality is really a desire for revenge, for violent leveling and upset (I, 361). Like revenge, the desire for equality knows no determinable limits, certainly none capable of finding fixed expression in law. And like revenge, it does not look to consequences; it is self-extinguishing. The right to equality is indissolubly attached to attacks on property, Bentham explained; and because he admitted no absolute distinction between luxury and subsistence, he anticipated that where enthusiasm for equality prevailed, presently there would be nothing left to divide: "All would shortly be destroyed" (*TL*,

p. 99). The desire for equality is simply destructive. It is asceticism. Indeed, revolutionary asceticism is uniquely despotic, for it seeks to deny pleasure to others. It would enforce standards which, if generally practiced, would disappoint every expectation. The monks at least kept their mortification to themselves.

The motives for asceticism are diverse, then, but ascetics have in common a peculiar sort of hope which gives to every type of asceticism the character of utility misapplied, rather than utility's opposite. Asceticism rejects common pleasures, and it pretends to overcome the psychology by which these pleasures are anticipated. But it nonetheless promises satisfactions of its own. Ordinarily, men act to satisfy expectations they hold of some future advantage, Bentham thought. They derive these expectations from social experiences, and although the gains they seek may not be moderate ones, they are part of ordinary use and available to common understanding. Expectations, then, are based on a view of the world in which there is a generally objective, short-term, and predictable proportion between exertion and reward. Asceticism, by contrast, views the prevailing relation between effort and reward as arbitrary and wholly unworthy. Still, it too anticipates reward, and on that account is not truly the adverse of utility. The ascetic counts the present as "but a point" and renounces present pleasures for future ones. Renunciation is, of course, part of every normal decision to put off satisfaction, but the ascetic takes a peculiarly dramatic view of the future. In this view, reward comes after death, or only to future generations, and the reward promised is unlike any men presently pursue. And, finally, the way to it appears to be free of every sort of labor required by utility, for typically no ordinary observations or calculations are part of the ascetic's efforts. In short, asceticism is apolitical; it is apocalyptic. In this sense, the ascetic disposition constitutes a deliberate and emphatic flight from utility.

According to Bentham's account, asceticism is subjective, antisocial, and above all antimodern. Each of these qualities prevents it from serving as a rationale for law, but the last is most important. And religious, philosophic, and revolutionary asceticism share this antimodern character. Whatever the purpose behind its rejection of contemporary values, asceticism may recommend and certainly results in cessation of ordinary business. This is the case with some experimental communities that have tried to transform men and change their pleasures; these are manifestly reactionary. It is the case too with asceticism as a general principle, for asceticism would sap the sources of natural wealth, "cramping commerce" (I, 5). Revolutionary fanatics especially would "pass the plane" over all ranks of society, property, and industry (Stark, III, 86). The consistent application of asceticism would turn earth into hell.

Asceticism appears to most men, then, as pure self-denial, and the consequence of persisting in it is just that. It cannot serve as a consistent rationale for law, because it denies men's subjection to the empire of pleasure and pain. Bentham could discover only one instance where asceticism was applied to the business of government—Sparta—and he explained that case by pointing to the peculiar requirements for the city's security.[9] But apart from this singular and compelling purpose, asceticism must fail as a rationale for law. It ignores the strength of expectations. It cannot justify legislation to the community, for no standard is generally practicable which reorders men's pleasures, or puts gratification off to some unforeseeable time, or, worse still, reserves happiness entirely for future generations. For most men, asceticism can have no appeal. It offers nothing to compensate them for their present disappointment. It is unenforceable.

Bentham's remarks on asceticism in *An Introduction* take on added political import with his attack on the French Declaration of the Rights of Man and Citizen in *Anarchical Fallacies.* The Declaration was, he insisted, an invitation to fanaticism. Not everyone who revolts against government is fanatic, of course, and Bentham spared the authors of the Declaration this epithet. The Jacobin is, though, and the Declaration speaks to men of that peculiarly despotic disposition (X, 296). The revolutionary fanatic shares the religious ascetic's apocalyptic vision and the philosophic ascetic's denunciation of contemporary values and his pride. The arrogance of the Declaration, in particular the alleged universalism of the rights it pronounced, was apparent enough, Bentham thought. Less apparent was its asceticism. The revolutionary fanatic was precisely a seer of the type described—ready to sacrifice indiscriminately whatever advantages social life presently holds for himself and existing generations, for the sake of the species (I, 360).

Like all rhetorical formulae, the French declaration of natural rights was antilegal. Bentham applied to natural rights the same argument he used against every higher-law standard: rhetorical formulae have nothing to contribute to the real business of legislation. The questions men "study to avoid" must be asked: what specific offense the law addresses, exactly who is hurt and helped by the law, and in what measure. The "right to property" must be limited, modified, and given detailed content before it can serve to secure possessions. In the case of natural rights, Bentham had this to say in addition: natural rights are especially apt slogans for the revolutionary fanatic because their effect is so clearly destructive. They are employed to repudiate contemporary values where these are embodied in existing laws. The whole work of natural rights is to declare legislation void. Even if natural rights are intended to serve as a rationale for revolution instead of legislation, they fail. They are, again, destructive, and offer a reason for beginning revolutions, but not for stopping them (I, 154). They provide no basis for establishing order where none exists, for they hold out hopes that cannot be fulfilled by any conceivable legal practice. The right to liberty, or the pursuit of happiness, will always be imperfect where there is government and law (*Correspondence,* I, 342; I, 303, 311). In particular, the leveling that produced equality in the first instance cannot be preserved by any conceivable system of law; it can only be sustained by the same means that established it in the first place—an army of inquisitors and executioners (I, 312). Bentham offered a litany of the logical and practical reasons why it is impossible to effect natural rights. Natural rights are, in short, rhetorical extravagances. They do not look to consequences. They are such that men cannot see to the end of them (II, 494). The only predictable outcome of claims to natural rights is perpetual insurrection.

The reason for the wholly antilegal character of natural rights goes beyond the fallacious reasoning they encourage and the consequences of this reasoning in practice. The despotic disposition that inspires appeals to natural rights is also responsible. Revolutionary fanaticism is one expression of a despotic disposition that simply cannot be argued with. And revolutionary fanaticism is the best contemporary proof that when this disposition takes to political action it is purely destructive. It is ascetic.

Unlike asceticism, which is utility "misapplied," aestheticism is not a principle at all; it is sheer caprice. The aesthete approves or disapproves of actions simply because he finds himself disposed to do so (I, 7-8). The only counsel he takes is of his own feelings and taste, or his "sympathies" and "antipathies." The various formulae Bentham called aesthetic—among them moral sense, common sense, natural law, and understanding—have this in common: they point to feelings only, and not to any external standard, to justify laws. They do not require men to examine the circumstances or consider the consequences of the measures proposed. Aestheticism is sheer spontaneity. It may be exactly what twentieth-century aestheticism boasts of being, then, pure self-expression. In this case, the divide between normalcy and insanity is obscured, though in this case too the aesthete's behavior is idiosyncratic and generally harmless. Bentham wrote of Robert Owen, whom he evidently came to view in something like this light: he "begins in vapour, and ends in smoke . . . He built some small houses; and people, who had no houses of their own, went to live in those houses—and he calls this success" (X, 570). More often, however, the feelings appealed to to justify action and especially legislation are shared. King James I conceived a violent antipathy against Arians, two of whom he burnt; Bentham wrote, "This gratification he procured himself without much difficulty: the notions of the time were favourable to it." The same king also hated tobacco, but was constrained from burning Sir Walter Raleigh in the fire with the Arians because this hatred was not so general (I, 10n.).

Bentham interested himself, of course, in appeals to shared feelings and tastes. He acknowledged that there need not be an "avowed, much less a constant opposition" between the prescriptions of aestheticism and those of utility (I, 8n.). After all, sympathies and antipathies result from experience, and social experiences are seldom unique: "What all men are exposed to suffer by, all men will be disposed to hate" (I, 10). For this reason, current penal legislation approximates the measures utility would recommend (I, 10). Aestheticism and utility recommend the same legal measures only coincidentally, however; their concurrence is not dependable. Utility too takes its content from men's feelings, but its consideration of sympathies and antipathies is exhaustive; and it also takes into account the circumstances and consequences of the measures contemplated. In matters of legislation, it is not enough to know that men suffer, Bentham repeated; legislators must ascertain what it is they suffer from, and predict what laws will relieve their misery. Aestheticism, by contrast, invites men to project the cause of their misery and remedies for it where they will. It is not surprising, then, that aestheticism does not inquire into "remote and imperceptible mischiefs." Bentham's classification of offenses is above all a reaction against this sort of subjectivism. Aestheticism is altogether remote from utility's world of calculation and detail. It is disdainful of the "statistical function," which is inseparable from utility, and this is sufficient by itself to make aestheticism antilegal.

Aestheticism's formulae disregard the requirements of legislation in practice. They also differ from utility, Bentham thought, because they are expressions of a despotic disposition. The aesthetic disposition inclines to severity (I, 10). This is clearly the case where punishment is concerned and antipathy is the rule. It is also true when it comes to designating offenses in the first place. If feelings alone determine what constitutes an offense, then every incident, however trivial, every difference of opinion and taste, is sufficient cause for naming men not only enemies but criminals as well (I, 10). Aestheticism is evidently a longing for unanimity. The desire to see one's own sentiments universally enforced is its mark; aestheticism is fundamentally the disposition of one who believes himself to be among the elect (I, 9n.). Virtue in legislators is no antidote to this severity, Bentham insisted; indeed "virtue" commonly directs men to deprive others of their pleasures, as asceticism shows (II, 254-255). Nor does ordinary benevolence mitigate aestheticism's severity. "It requires a highly enlightened benevolence," Bentham wrote, "an uncommon philosophy, in order to sympathize with tastes which are not our own" (I, 375). Aestheticism brings with it intolerance, and neither good character nor benevolence is a remedy for this accompaniment of a despotic disposition. Tolerance is more often a personal quality belonging to those who employ the principle of utility, but in any case, tolerance is the consequence of a calculating disposition in practice. That was utility's great promise—objectivity, and the peace it is supposed to bring.

Men justify their actions and laws by appealing to their feelings only where they are not required to observe any other standard, Bentham thought—where, that is, they do not need to seek concurrence. Caprice is the mark of all men who hold irresponsible power. And it has been the basis of most established systems of law. Still, he connected aestheticism with one class and one sort of law in particular (I, 8). If asceticism is the disposition that belongs to moralists and revolutionary fanatics, aestheticism is the characteristic disposition of the aristocracy and its allies. It is the disposition of political men who concur already among themselves and whose political discussions proceed by appeals to shared sentiments. This describes the condition of the English aristocracy at the time of the Glorious Revolution, Bentham wrote by way of example, when a successful appeal was made to the doctrine of the original contract because "men were too obviously and too generally interested in the observance of these rules, to entertain doubts concerning the force of any arguments they saw employed in their support" (I, 269).

Aestheticism is politically important when it takes counsel not of feelings simply but of taste, which is not purely personal. Twentieth-century aestheticism, which applauds individual self-expression, is misleading in this context, for taste is the common property of the arbiters of sensibility, the aristocracy (IX, 45-46). And it would be clearly self-contradictory to pretend that aestheticism could be a universal rationale for law, for taste is exclusive to the aristocracy. Where taste is concerned, each man does not count for one. "Bad taste" is a familiar political epithet, Bentham pointed out, and in aesthetic politics, disgust and political opposition are indistinguishable (IX, 46). Further, by good taste the aristocracy meant a special set of preferences. Taste referred to the sympathies and notions given men by culture, that is, classical education. Bentham, who rejected everything classical, took as his chief antagonist in this matter of aestheticism William Blackstone. His choice of opponent shows the continuity that existed in his mind between aristocratic political conservatism and legal conservatism, and the common basis for both of these in the form of despotic disposition he called aesthetic.

Bentham's purpose in *A Fragment on Government* was to "undeceive the timid and admiring student" for whom Blackstone was the authority on English law and the constitution (I, 295). Bentham proceeded, therefore, to expose the logical confusion, meaninglessness, and deliberate obfuscation that marked the commentator's rhetorical dazzle. Timidity and admiration would not be easily overcome, he knew. For one thing, Blackstone's work was expository; it was designed to help students learn the law, and not to criticize or change it. And when it comes to learning, utility's language—the language of logic and sensation—simply does not have the same appeal. As for utility's prescriptions, they are similarly tedious. Utility's truths will not "compress themselves into epigrams," Bentham wrote, and men are very much "governed by the ear" (I, v, 236, 232). Even so, Blackstone's rhetoric could be shown to be self-serving, and his ideas shown to be calculated to advance the interests of the legal profession; Bentham's criticisms on this score are discussed in Chapters 4 and 6. More important, for now, is his observation that ambitious youths even of the "democratical section" emulate the tastes and opinions of the aristocracy (IX, 45-46) and take Blackstone as their model. There is something more to Blackstone's rhetoric than fallacious reasoning in the service of sinister interests. Rhetorical dazzle does not simply conceal these interests, Bentham recognized, it is integral to them. Rhetoric is not, in this case, purely instrumental. It does more than make conservatism palatable; it is precisely what is to be preserved. For aestheticism is distinguished by attention to manners, expression, and eloquence in particular—these are the marks of culture. It is not surprising, then, that Bentham did not always attack Blackstone's conservative political preferences directly, but chose to attack his classicism as well. Blackstone "taught Jurisprudence to speak the language of the Scholar and Gentleman . . . [he] has decked her out . . . to advantage, from the toilette of classic erudition; enlivened her with metaphors and allusions;

and sent her abroad in some measure to instruct, and in still greater measure to entertain, the most miscellaneous and even the most fastidious societies" (I, 236). Aestheticism justifies actions by appealing to shared tastes and uses ideas taken from antiquity in this cause.

Aristocratic aestheticism makes Athens, Sparta, and Venice the measure of all things, Bentham explained. Blackstone appealed in typical fashion to ancient authors and to classical virtues in order to understand and reconcile himself to British laws and the constitution. It is within this received ideological framework that political affairs and political discussion move. Either the present order is eulogized for comprising the mix of virtues recommended by the ancients, or it is charged with corrupting the classical standard of perfection and a return to origins is urged. But the taste and affections that culture inspires are simply inadequate for understanding or practicing politics, Bentham argued, and this is especially true of legislation. If he called men corrupt, his tone was one of irony and not virtue offended. And he did not use corruption to refer to the upset of an ideal constitutional mix or balance. Bentham leveled his attacks against Whig and Tory alike. He did seem to take his stand between them, though, and it turned on this very matter of aestheticism. He appeared to despise the great families more. The crown employed "influence" (and Bentham objected to its abuse), but at least the crown used rewards and appealed to men's passions, particularly "ostentatious ambition," to get the day-to-day business of state done. Were it not for the "children of corruption," the business of government would stagnate, for where aestheticism prevails, as it does in the case of country gentlemen, there is little concern for business at all (I, 281). Instead, politics is perceived in terms of character and the preservation of forms. Gentlemen profess to love virtue and to think that it is character that determines the nature of political order. And they persist in viewing these as adequate terms for justifying political measures, even technical administrative ones like salary levels.[10] Aestheticism makes use of classical notions in this way, Bentham understood, because the aristocracy is interested above all in stability. In this respect, aestheticism is a flight from utility and, he thought, self-defeating. There is nothing permanent in the world, and men must be reconciled to it as he himself was. Classical formulae are the best evidence that the aristocracy persists in an ideal alien to contemporary political experience. Indeed, a second ideological refuge for aestheticism is similarly a mark of this class's reluctance to confront the necessity for change.

Classicism is one source of aestheticism's formulae, but aestheticism finds the language and instruments of stability in the common law as well. Now, preoccupation with stability, which directs men's affections to antiquity and to common law, is not the same as either reverence for tradition or ·prescription, Bentham took care to emphasize. In Britain sentiments attach to the common law, which is evidently not identical with custom or ancient usage (II, 596-598). Common law is more than experience, but less than science. It is, Bentham argued, the worst of both worlds. Changes in the common law are not the result of slow accretions of collective experience, but neither are they deductions from a consistently applicable principle. Changes in the common law are unpredictable, and they occur case by case. Common law simply does not offer the certainty that custom guarantees. It succeeds in avoiding neither blind routine nor everything arbitrary (I, 161). The whole system, Bentham maintained in a phrase now famous, is based on that peculiarly English growth, legal fictions (IX, 59). The point about legal fictions in this context is what they share with ideas drawn from classical thought: for Bentham both are inspired by a concern for stability and both fail in their object.

Fictions are deliberate falsehoods, but it is not their untruth that chiefly disturbed Bentham; discourse of every kind requires fictions.[11] For example, since it is never possible to know for certain whether a particular law or judicial ruling suits a new exigency, the best men can do is to proceed by analogy; legislation is prediction. The common law goes further than this, however. It is typical of aestheticism in that it uses fictions to avoid asking about the suitability of measures directly. The whole object of common-law fictions is to avoid the appearance of expedience and change. Legal fictions too, then, are a flight from utility. Because of its subjectivism and the fictions to which sentiments attach, aestheticism prevents men from learning anything from the actual events of the world, Bentham warned. The consequence is that even where the common law aims at *salus respublica,* and not at advancing the special interests of the legal profession or its aristocratic allies, it is bound to overshoot or fall short of its mark (*OLG,* p. 194n.). Bentham was never loath to point out the sinister interests served by means of legal fictions, of course. But he also remarked on their failure to serve these or any interests consistently in the modern state.

Aestheticism uses fictions to escape the politics of expedience now practiced, for the most part, by economic men. All of the ideas which aestheticism commonly appeals to in its efforts to ensure stability— among them natural law, original contract, and ancient constitution—

are fictions. Government itself is a fiction, Bentham cautioned; it is not "there" or absolute at all; government comprises a variety of relations which are in continual flux and subject to innumerable conditions, like all other relations (I, 263). The political import of Bentham's favorite term, "fiction," is evident: fictions provide no firm ground for politics. The stability sought by these means is entirely illusory. Even if aestheticism succeeds in its ambition of unanimity, and these fictions become the objects of general affection, it has not done all that stability requires. For men have political objectives beyond the obedience that is thought to accompany political unanimity; it is not enough, Bentham wrote, that the system "prevents a scramble" (II, 597).[12] In any case, fictions cannot protect men against change and the political disputes change causes, and they cannot really satisfy the aesthete's longing for fixed objects for his affections. In the end, they are not only self-serving, but also self-deluding. Indeed, the two are inseparable: "It is an old story," Bentham observed, "how Interest smooths the road to Faith" (I, 269). In short, fictions perpetuate the mistaken notion that political agreement is possible only where men share a common culture. This notion is despotic and simply impracticable.

Bentham employed all the familiar eighteenth-century arguments against custom proper. Men owe nothing to the collective experience of the past, and certainly nothing when it comes to laws:

Those who duly consider upon what slight and trivial circumstances, even in the happiest times, the adoption or rejection of a Law so often turns . . . those who consider the desolate and abject state of the human intellect, during the periods in which so great a part of the still subsisting mass of institutions had their birth . . . will not be quite so zealous, perhaps, as our Author [Blackstone] has been, to terrify men from setting up what is now "private judgment," against what was once "public." (I, 231)

If asceticism mortgages the present for the future, custom sacrifices "the real interests of the living to the imaginary interests of the dead"; it is not, in short, rationally self-interested (II, 399). Despite the disadvantages they have in common, the political conservatism characteristic of aestheticism is quite remote from reverence for tradition, and Bentham pointed to common law to make this clear. Aestheticism's position is more aptly described as "antipathy to reform," and traditions are cited merely to enforce that antipathy (*OLG*, p. 109). Blackstone warned that every alteration in the law is regretted afterward, but, Bentham observed, Blackstone was himself a critic of the common law. In fact, the expositor did not ward off changes in the law, only rude and arrogant censoring of the law (I, 230). Political and legal aestheticism share this, then: they connect stability less with custom than with popular obedience, indeed obsequiousness. Bentham attacked aestheticism for its antipopular character. Often, however, his insights into aestheticism were subtler than this purely political charge first suggests. The aristocracy is not simply opposed to the people, he thought, it is torn between two worlds (as Chapter 6 explains in some detail). This tension is plain in aristocrats' political discourse and in their political affairs, and it can be seen wherever their fictions are employed. The aristocracy is torn between disdain for the people—for men who live outside of culture—and dependence upon them. Aestheticism's formulae are designed to camouflage this conflict. For one thing, aestheticism is caught between the prejudice that subservience to authority constitutes stability and the view that consent is the only possible basis of modern politics. The fiction of an original contract, to take one example, is a recipe for just this sort of political indeterminacy; the "latent virtue" of a fictional contract is that it can be used either to loose or to bind men to authority. Blackstone's rhetoric, Bentham showed in *A Fragment on Government,* can be employed to encourage either revolt or obedience (I, 286). Aesthetic formulae are calculated to avoid confronting political questions directly. Bentham wrote of the notion of a contract: "men were more ready to deem themselves qualified to judge when it was such a promise was *broken,* then to decide directly and avowedly on the delicate question, when it was that a King acted so far in *opposition* to the happiness of his People, that it were better no longer to obey him" (I, 269). In each instance the aesthete decides the question he "studies to avoid" by whether his feeling of disdain for or dependence on the people is stronger. Aestheticism is the mark of men who exercise irresponsible power; but it is nonetheless the mark of a weak system and insecure men. Asceticism is enthusiastic; aestheticism is not fanatic, only capricious. Still, nothing in weakness, passivity, or ennervation, Bentham observed, makes aestheticism less despotic.

Asceticism and revolutionary fanaticism, which is its current political expression, and aestheticism and antipathy to reform are despotic dispositions and antilegal ideologies. Bentham opposed both revolutionary democracy and political conservatism, though the precise sequence of his arguments against each remains a matter of historical research.[13] He was consistent, however, in seeing that the two attitudes and political preferences had certain things in common. Both were marked by fallacious reasoning. Both employed rhetorical formulae that prevented application to details, the real business of legislation (I, 303). For Bentham, there was no distinguishing between the spirit and the letter of the law (II, 318-319). Modernization of laws and institutions requires this close attention, and modernization, rather than any particular form of government, was his chief concern. Further, both asceticism and aestheticism represent a despotic disposition that makes utilitarian concerns simply impossible. Asceticism and aestheticism characterize men who insist upon unanimity for the political values they espouse. This above all makes them antilegal attitudes. In every one of his writings, Bentham's main theme was good government. He did not go so far as to promote the notion of strong states, however, a notion which resists every comparison of political institutions except for their efficiency. For utility values the happiness of individuals, and this is only possible where no one and no desires are denied a place in the legislator's calculations. Sympathy for reform is one condition of good government, but not the only one. Toleration is another—toleration, or at least the absence of a despotic disposition that is self-serving and above all unconciliatory. Asceticism and aestheticism are unaccommodating.

Of the two ideologies, Bentham gave more attention to aestheticism, for the prevailing political attitude was resistance to reform. He knew, however, that the discourse characteristic of aristocratic politics does not constitute all there is to contemporary politics, even where it is not revolutionary. There remains too the political tradition of absolutism, which raised in a plain manner the questions of authority and obedience that aestheticism tried to obscure. Bentham's differences with this tradition were not often the focus of his writings, but they were important for his purpose, nonetheless; no state theorist can ignore entirely the matters that go under the name of sovereignty. Bentham's reflections on sovereignty are the subject of the next chapter.

4. Sovereignty and Law

The season of *Fiction* is now over. (I, 269)

Sovereignty was not always, or exclusively, an attribute of kingship; in addition, some state theorists granted the title "sovereign" to the state itself. Reason of state was still conceived in the traditional way, as a set of practical imperatives imposed on rulers by every exercise of power. But at the same time, reason of state was taken by some to refer to the "will" of the state, constrained to preserve itself and maximize its power. Government was distinct from the state, in this view; it was a way of organizing power to give the state's will effect. Naturalism, in short, was displaced from a psychology of the individual to a psychology of the state-person. Not every state theorist contributed to this disquieting development, however, and Bentham did so only with the greatest reluctance and care. He preferred to speak of "political society" rather than "state," and he did not distinguish political society from government consistently or to any clear purpose. Even where he wrote about government in instrumental terms, as a matter of technique for arriving at utility, it was not the power of the state-person governors exercised, and only rarely did Bentham say that it was the will of the state governors effected. Rulers are servants of the people, he wrote in contradiction to a famous pronouncement characterizing rulers as servants of the state (IX, 43). Bentham's reason for not personifying the state is clear—he wanted to emphasize the state's basis in individualism. He wanted rulers especially to recall that political order is constituted of diverse and changeable relations among individuals.

The moral status of the state, Bentham judged, was threatened equally by the old metaphor of the body politic with one sovereign head and by the more recent notion of the sovereign state. Power was not something that attached to the person of rulers, he advised, and his rejection of the long-standing division between civil and criminal law in favor of distributive and penal law constituted an attack on this vestige of monarchical sovereignty (IX, 8-9). But power did not belong to the fictional state-person either. Power consists of a relation of obedience between ruler and ruled, a relation that is particular in every case and entirely changeable. Bentham argued against the prevalent contrast between the state of nature and political society, and explained that government is not "absolute"; government too consists of relationships among individuals, and subsists or not with reference to them and their activities in particular. With respect to different persons and objects, he wrote, men can be said to be in more or less of a condition of political society. The presence or absence of a "habit of obedience" may be difficult to discern (I, 263), and the disposition to obedience is liable to innumerable modifications and may change from day to day (*OLG,* p. 18n.). Bentham's ideological message is unmistakable: it is only on account of the happiness of individuals that government exists. His words were directed first of all at political men, and to them he wrote that the interest of the community is "the sum of the interests of the several members who compose it" (I, 2). The end of government ought to be their happiness, personally and severally. Wherever possible, Bentham employed the language of social relations to describe political ones: public services are only one of a multitude of services individuals perform for one another, he advised. He was sensitive, of course, to the special character of political activity, and for just this reason, he wanted men to recall that political activity is nonetheless a service. In the same vein, he objected to the "false and obscure" notion of the sacrifice of private to public interest (*TL,* p. 145), and was perfectly consistent in saying that not even rulers have to be philanthropic. Their happiness too must be considered, and government ought to be organized to provide real rewards for their services. Utility, or each state's higher rationality, is a middle ground constituted in every case of the special interaction between the ruler's right to satisfaction and the happiness of subjects. Each state, in this view, has its own utility, but he denied to the state its own "person." Bentham's state theory is incomprehensible apart from his treatment of the concepts associated with every personification of the state: the "body politic," the "general will," and the central idea of state theory—"sovereignty." These were all deliberately abandoned or altered to suit Bentham's own purpose (I, 2; II, 332; IV, 544). The place of "sovereignty" in his work is the focus of this chapter and the next.

Bentham refused to accept as supreme the claims of the sovereign monarch or the sovereign state. Nevertheless, the notion of sovereignty was by no means absent from his writings. Although he had recourse to it often and variously, two principal uses stand out. Prominent in Bentham's thought is the notion of popular sovereignty. He used it in a fashion consistent with the part sovereignty traditionally played in state theory as a normative idea. Sovereignty was meant to draw attention to the special origin of power and to justify the special nature of power—its absolute and innovative nature. The main point of the first section below is that with popular sovereignty, Bentham advocated absolutism, even though he rejected its monarchical form. Sovereignty also makes its appearance in Bentham's juristic formula "law is an expression of the sovereign's will"; and his command theory is the subject of the second section below. The familiarity enjoyed by the command theory of law has made the connection between this limited and purely formal notion of sovereignty and the sovereignty of state theory appear indissoluble, and their purposes appear the same. They arc not. Sovereignty is required by command theory on logical grounds alone: where law is defined as an expression of will, there must be one designable person or body whose will is expressed. In state theory, by contrast, sovereignty is not a logical requirement at all, but a norm of order.

Sovereignty, as is explained below, was not a simple idea. Historically, the practical object of the designation "sovereign" was obtaining obedience;[1] where several authorities competed for supremacy, and where the way power was exercised was through law, one authority claimed legal omnipotence. And in order to achieve this political objective of reconciling men to parochial absolutism, sovereignty provided a theoretical account of the origin and nature of power. The command theory of law, however, simply assumes both political parochialism and the existence of a designable sovereign. It offers no solution to the problem of competing authorities; it does not broach the question of the origin or nature of power. Put strongly, the command theory of law does very little to advance our understanding of either sovereignty or law. The question it does address, with its emphasis on the source of law, is the formal one of a law's validity. Even though command theory was propagated by those who valued obedience and feared disorder, it was not designed, as sovereignty was, to reconcile the subjects of power to it. After all, the validity of a law says little of interest to those called upon to obey. Bentham's command theory is typically limited and formalistic. But he directed command theory chiefly at the legal profession—which is quite properly concerned with validity. And Bentham did not appeal to the formulae of command theory to avoid consideration of the content of law or political preferences generally. His thoughts on sovereignty and law are considered here in the context of his state theory. Bentham's discussion of the sovereignty of the state is distinct from both popular sovereignty and the sovereign whose command is law, and it is reserved for the next chapter.

Popular Sovereignty

The essence of sovereignty, Bentham wrote, is constituted of obedience (II, 541). This statement asserts too much, for obedience is not quite the essence of sovereignty. Still, it provides a good beginning for a discussion of the historical part sovereignty played in state theory, and of its fate in Bentham's political thought. Obedience was indeed the practical object of kings in the era of the consolidation of monarchical absolutism, and sovereignty was part of the ideological apparatus employed for that purpose. The claim of sovereignty was not directed against the disobedience of individuals or against any resistance on utilitarian grounds. Sovereignty was principally brandished by kings first in their struggles with the universal church, and then against clericalism generally— against, that is, resistance threatened on religious grounds. Sovereignty was not entirely coincident with the notion of the divine right of kings, though. Every authority claimed its power by divine right; it was agreed that God commanded obedience to all constituted authorities and that no other origin of power was conceivable but God. The question sovereignty addressed was: which authority is supreme?[2] Kings claimed not only divine right to rule, then, but divine right to govern free of all earthly superiors. The sovereign was no one's subject. Bodin, the greatest early state theorist, characterized sovereignty as the "most high, absolute, and perpetual power." He meant that from the sovereign's exercise of power there is no appeal on earth; the sovereign power is an original superior power and not derivative.[3] For Bodin, the sovereign was not legally boundless, but he was irresistible.[4]

Nothing portrays the practical import of the title "sovereign" more graphically than the familiar image of the body politic with one head. The requirement of one head was, to begin with, a political one. Bodin determined that the divisions wrought by the French wars of religion in the sixteenth century required a new integrative force, and that order was unworkable apart from the rule of a single sovereign. From the start of its modern use, then, sovereignty was indissolubly attached to the person of kings. On the king's person turned one political invention critical for the development of the modern state—the distinction the "king's peace" and criminal law uniformly imposed between criminal and innocent. And on the king's personal connections and sympathies turned a second critical distinction which governed conduct in the modern state—the designation of men's status as subject or foreigner, and as foreign friend or enemy.

The language and disputes that provided the context for sovereignty were religious, and originally sovereignty had to be a religious idea, for only then could kings challenge clericalism and demand absolute obedience. Sovereignty rested, Bentham acknowledged in *A Fragment on Government,* on belief in the "metaphisico-legal impotence," or "enchantment," of subjects. He accused Blackstone of buttressing his preference for obedience to constituted authorities by adding a "theological flourish" to his otherwise utilitarian account of government. Blackstone "fetched the governors' endowments from the clouds" to bewilder and entrance men (I, 272); he wanted to see the people obsequious. Historically, the religious character of the sovereignty idea was not purely rhetorical, however. It pointed not only to the impracticability of resistance to kings, but also to the inconceivability of resistance. Bodin's argument for the sovereign monarch was based only in part on his political judgment that kings alone could keep order. His principal argument was theological. Hierarchy and the indivisibility of power, he believed, were norms that governed a divinely ordered universe. They ought to characterize the political sphere as they did creation generally. On account of this metaphysical view, sovereign and state were indistinguishable for Bodin. What sovereignty did was to raise the inexpedience of resistance to the level of iniquity; its essence lay here, in the inconceivability of order without supreme power. Sovereignty was a matter of belief and not of degree of force. It did not depend for its meaning simply on the strength of men's desire for peace or on the enforceability of the king's peace. Sovereignty was in practice separable from the king's power, which was, Bentham knew, like every claim of absolute power, an aspiration. Only after the theological origin of sovereignty was forgotten or obscured could political thinkers reduce sovereignty to a matter of organization—to a matter of effectively concentrating power in some part of government.[5]

Historically, then, the religious character of sovereignty was not simply rhetorical—part of an effort to relieve the restraints clericalism in particular imposed on kings. It had a theological basis and was a norm of order, as Bodin's thought demonstrates. Sovereignty's attachment to the person of kings must be viewed in this light, for this connection too had a theological basis and was not solely a matter of the power of kings in practice. Divine right said that God was the origin of political power. Sovereignty added that God determined the nature of power, and served as the model for its exercise. Sovereignty was impossible without a view of God which emphasized the creative power of His will. According to this model, will was a force that initiates and innovates. The king's expression of will was an imitation of God in several respects: because the king could do no wrong, because from his will there was no appeal, and above all because of the creative character attributed to his willing. Sovereignty was indistinguishable from the conviction that by acts of will kings could justifiably overturn the restraints of established moral and positive law, and that in doing so they were not acting simply destructively. There is no better example of an act of sovereignty than the one Bentham picked to characterize monarchical rule: mercy, he wrote, is an imitation of God (I, 529). The sovereign's will was an irresistible force for change, and equally—indeed on that account—for order. The sovereign's power was protean. It was also liable to slip into arbitrariness.

One phrase accurately sums up the several notions sovereignty comprised. It is the pronouncement that accompanied political acts under monarchical absolutism: *"tel est mon plaisir."* It proclaimed that from the sovereign's will there is no appeal; it demanded obedience. *"Tel est mon plaisir"* announced, further, that the sovereign's expression of "plaisir" is sufficient justification for every exercise of power. The phrase points to the traditional association of absolutism and arbitrariness, and the history of the sovereignty idea is the history of limiting absolutism and restraining arbitrariness. Certainly, Bentham was an opponent of caprice in politics. But it is equally true, and more instructive, to describe his thought as, in some respects at least, heir to the sovereignty idea. His constitutionalism was not a rejection of absolutism; his notion of utility made the pleasure of men generally the justification for every exercise of power and reconciled them to the irresistibility of innovation. Utility's history began with *"tel est mon plaisir."*

This is not evident, for Bentham was a vigorous opponent of monarchical absolutism—and ultimately of monarchy in any form. And he was concerned enough generally about checks on rulers that this concern can appear to exclude all others. Bentham often employed sovereignty synonymously with monarchy as a form of government and, for the most part, did not explore what sovereignty added to the idea of kingship. He was not insensitive to its religious character, though. The sovereign monarch is viewed as a sort of God, Bentham observed; the people "worship him," and he moves according to his pleasure (I, 529). Bentham's ambition was to combat the monarch's claim to have no interest but that of his people (III, 442). That the sovereign's interest is the nation's, especially in matters of wealth and war, he simply denied (IX, 137). The sovereign's interest coincides with the people's in the same way that the wolf's coincides with the sheep's, Bentham wrote, and he attacked monarchy as a system of established plunderage (VIII, 542; IX, 102, 112, 136, 141). The sovereign will "accumulate under his own grasp all the external instruments of felicity, all the objects of general desire . . . all at the expense of, and by the sacrifice of, the felicity of the other members of the community" (IX, 128). Here, Bentham took sovereignty as part of the ideology of monarchy, and did what others had done—turned sovereignty against itself by making the people and their happiness supreme. He raised the specter of sovereign kings in order that the recollection would add meaning and force to his notion of popular sovereignty.

Bentham did not present popular sovereignty as a form of government alternative to monarchy, however. His *Constitutional Code* prescribed unmixed representative democracy for modern states, but this should not obscure the distinct purpose of popular sovereignty in his thought. Representative democracy, Bentham sometimes claimed, is a logical consequence of utility; it is, he sometimes argued, his own political preference. But representative democracy is not a norm of order; Bentham could conceive of order without it. This is not the case with popular sovereignty. The idea that sovereignty resides "essentially in the nation" was neither radical nor new, Bentham insisted. It was "perfectly true, perfectly harmless, and perfectly uninstructive" (II, 504). It meant that government depends upon obedience. Obedience, he advised, is the "efficient cause of all power" (II, 541; *OLG*, p. 18n.). This is true for the most absolute monarchy as well as for the broadest democracy (II, 504). Popular sovereignty does not simply reverse sovereignty, in this view; the people originate power but they do not rule. Not even in his plan for a representative democracy did Bentham abandon the dichotomy between ruling few and subject many (IX, 106); that is why he also continued to use the title "sovereign" to describe the central governmental authority. Bentham's notion of popular sovereignty simultaneously emphasized the ruler-subject distinction that sovereignty was designed to make, and put it in doubt. Briefly, his purpose with popular sovereignty was to show that the power of the subject people is supreme and that it may operate as a restraint—though not necessarily a constitutional one—on rulers. The issue of the organization of government, he wrote in his *Constitutional Code,* is "how to prevent the sinister sacrifice" (IX, 49), and he would have the people choose and remove governors. But no institutional arrangement can substitute for an attitude of vigilance and suspicion on the part of the subject many, he knew, and popular sovereignty need not have any formal institutional expression. When he spoke of the sovereign people, Bentham meant not electors only, therefore, but everyone subject to rule—the laboring classes and the aristocracy as well (by contrast, he excluded the aristocracy from the public opinion tribunal in his *Constitional Code*). He rejected at the same time the contemporary use of the term "people" as the vulgar (II, 380) and Rousseau's impersonal "man in general." The consequence of ignoring the happiness of all men as the right end of government, he cautioned, is the possibility of resistance. The people are "judges with arms" (IX, 58-59). Bentham meant popular sovereignty to counter princely terror with the terror of the people. From their judgment, there is no appeal (II, 310).

This is not to say that Bentham was uniformly optimistic about the efficacy of popular self-defense against rulers. Popular sovereignty was no more a prediction of successful resistance against misrule in practice than traditional sovereignty was a guarantee of the king's efficacy in securing obedience. If the multitude were "clamorous and unruly" (I, 230), this is not the same as being possessed of a "faculty of effectual resistance" (II, 287); and he often spoke of the people as "blinded, deluded, unsuspicious, uninquisitive, and ever too patient" (III, 439; IX, 112). Further, Bentham characteristically pointed to the power of people, and not "the people," to disobey, and it is useful here to recall that his notion of popular sovereignty is not entirely like Rousseau's. Rousseau wrote of "the people," who act together in defense of a moral order created for them by a Legislator. They are guardians.[6] In Bentham's view, there is no common signal for the grounds of disobedience. "For that which shall serve as a particular sign to each particular person, I have already given one—his own internal persuasion of a balance of *utility* on the side of resistance" (I, 287-288). No ritual of agreement ever marks the formation of political society, for Bentham, and no embodiment of common interest like the general will defends it. Popular sovereignty is plainly a matter of self-defense in practice, a matter of each subject's independent will to resist government when it acts in opposition to the happiness of subjects. Bentham did not actually recommend resistance, nor did he indicate under what conditions he would advise it. His concern was to justify resistance, and this normative purpose is clear. For when it came to resistance, he wrote that private individuals should consider the interest of the community generally, while ordinarily the principle of utility recommends prudence to private men and restricts considerations of public utility to rulers. Utility, he urged here, makes disobedience possible; it provides all men with a "guide through these straits." Still, Bentham acknowledged, popular sovereignty finds expression most often in vigilance rather than revolution; the whole point of good government is that grievances are remediable, and the motto of subjects should be: "To obey punctually; to censure freely" (I, 230).

Popular sovereignty meant more to Bentham than a repudiation of monarchy, and it meant more, even, than a restraint imposed on every exercise of power by the necessity of winning the acquiescence of the people. Like sovereignty before it, popular sovereignty was a normative idea. The possibility of resistance was the chief consequence of popular sovereignty, but defense of resistance was not its only or main contribution to political thought. Popular sovereignty explains not only the origin but also the nature of power; it justifies absolutism. And Bentham knew that popular sovereignty strengthened absolutism as never before. Absolutism refers, of course, to the extent of the rulers' field of authority. It is entirely compatible with constitutionalism; division of power is evidence of a distrust of absolute power but not a rejection of it.[7] Bentham's constitutionalism provided checks on absolute power, but it did not limit it (IX, 160). His *Constitutional Code* aimed at preventing the "sinister sacrifice"; significantly, it left unimpaired the will and the power to perform any acts conducive to the right end of government (IX, 49, 62; I, 288). Bentham could not have presented his prescription for abolutism more boldly. The supreme legislature in this scheme is "omnicompetent" (IX, 160 119-124). Its local field of service is coextensive with the territory of the state, he wrote; its logical field of service is coextensive with the field of human action (IX, 160). Further, no method or instrument is categorically denied governors in their exercise of power. And this is all true because sovereignty resides with the people. Sovereignty and constitutionalism were at odds not so much over absolutism, then, as over arbitrariness, and the contention that Bentham was heir to the sovereignty idea cannot rest by pointing to his recommendation of absolutism; it must consider too this matter of arbitrariness.

Arbitrariness is not a simple notion. Bentham observed that arbitrariness was associated with caprice, and he understood why. Not personal desires but the unpredictability of these desires is what makes caprice arbitrary. No one, he wrote, can foresee the course of caprice (I, 325). The essence of arbitrariness is uncertain change. Clearly, Bentham looked upon the personal pleasure of individuals as the rationale for law; this was utility's object. He rejected caprice, however. He did not accept as justification for political conduct any expression of desire that did not look to consequences and that was unpredictable. Arbitrariness, or uncertainty about the course of desire, is what makes caprice anathema to every legalist, Bentham included. Mercy is an imitation of God, he remarked, and added that it belongs to the vocabulary of tyranny, for it can only be in opposition to and at the expense of justice (I, 529). It is worth noting that arbitrariness is not exclusively a legal issue. Deviation from established rules makes the unpredictability, or arbitrariness, of an action clear, of course, but it is not only in contrast to laws that arbitrariness gets its character. And nothing in legal procedures or in the generality of a law per se saves these from being capricious; Bentham's attack on aestheticism makes this point plainly. Like any other action, legislation can have its basis in desires that do not look to consequences and whose purpose and course are thus uncertain. The main point is that traditionally sovereignty was not necessarily opposed to legalism. Sovereignty did not imply a rejection of legal forms or procedures; sovereigns typically exercised their power through law. And the notion of the unity of sovereignty through different reigns—of the perpetuity of sovereign power—was a great step in political thought, Bentham recognized; it was crucial in establishing what has come to be the "uniform and universal" expectation of continuity in the law (*OLG,* pp. 65-66n.). True, where sovereignty is an accepted idea, and *"tel est mon plaisir"* justifies every exercise of power, the total predictability that is supposed to accompany customary routines is not assured. But the purpose of the sovereignty idea was precisely to introduce the irresistibility of change into politics by modeling power on God's will, and political expectations came to embrace innovation. Although *"tel est mon plaisir"* can slip into arbitrariness, arbitrariness was not a mark of the sovereignty idea; sovereignty did not inevitably point to uncertain or unpredictable change, only to innovation. Bentham wanted to eliminate caprice from rule. He accepted absolutism, however, and he accepted too the necessity for innovation. Confronted with the sort of resistance to change that labels every reform as "arbitrariness," Bentham reacted vehemently, and even felt compelled to appeal to heaven to combat this view: "God forbid!" (I, 290). Uncertainty, he pointed out, is as likely to be the result of opposition to change and of constraints on power as of absolute power (I, 325). Chief among legalists, Bentham urged that only with change is security possible, and he was satisfied with the "defeasible perpetuity" of legislation. Innovation was irresistible because order is based on diverse and changeable desires—on happiness; this was always true, but here it was transformed into a principle of order.

If sovereignty was not necessarily characterized by arbitrariness, it nonetheless established politics that had for its content and rationale nothing but the expression and satisfaction of desires. Historically, sovereignty used the image of God to assure men that expressions of desire and exercises of will were creative forces for order. This work has been obscured by the depersonalization of the sovereignty idea. Once sovereignty's task of introducing pleasure and change into political expectations had been completed, pleasure generally replaced *"mon plaisir,"* and the personal character of sovereignty was eliminated. There was then no longer any reason for sovereignty to attach to kings, rather than to people generally. Hobbes, for example, appealed to the metaphor of the body politic with one head to add force to his recommendation of monarchical government, but monarchy had become, in his hands, a purely political preference. Sovereign kingship was never simply a matter of who could best keep order, though; the assignment of sovereignty to kings was based originally on a metaphysical view of the universe which required unified rule. Once popular sovereignty replaced this view, the notion of a unified sovereign was maintained chiefly by those who advanced a command theory of law, and their reasons were formal, as the next section explains.

When Bentham wrote of popular sovereignty, he did not refer directly to the theological origin of the idea; he did not call the voice of the people the voice of God. But he did use popular sovereignty to account for the origin and absolute nature of power. With popular sovereignty, he declared politics to be the expression and satisfaction of desires, he recognized will as a creative force for order, and he admitted the irresistibility of innovation. Popular sovereignty expresses itself in two ways, Bentham thought—in resistance to rulers, or self-defense; and, where political society is organized to give it full expression, in law. For in modern states especially, every exercise of power reveals the constraints of popular sovereignty, and legislation is no exception. This is not to say, however, that popular sovereignty and utility are coincident. Bentham never said they were. Popular sovereignty is no better insurance against arbitrariness than sovereignty was traditionally. It means only that from the will of the people there is no appeal. Though the course of men's desires may be arbitrary, it is not inevitably so, and the individual will remains the only possible force for order. For Bentham, utility is the higher rationality that proceeds from the diverse and conflicting wills of individuals, and its institutional expression is a unified system of law. Sovereignty, he wrote optimistically, shows itself only in compositions (IX, 5; *TL,* p. 445).

It remains to distinguish Bentham's notion of popular sovereignty from two allied but theoretically distinct ideas: unified government and the "constituent power of the people." In contrast to popular sovereignty, neither unified government nor popular elections were normative ideas for Bentham. At times, he presented both of them as logical or practical requirements of utility, but not as absolute values; they were purely instrumental. This is most clearly the case with unified government. Bentham sometimes employed "sovereignty" to indicate a way of organizing government, where one person or body has the office of assigning and distributing to other officials their departments, determining their conduct, and on occasion acting in their stead. This role historically attached to monarchs, he knew, but the part could also be taken by legislative assemblies.[8] The point is that sovereignty here is descriptive of an office, and not normative. An offense against sovereignty in this context is one among other offenses against the operations of government, Bentham wrote, and it may be a peculiarly effective sort of mischief, but it is mischief and not *lèse-majesté.* Nor is this way of organizing government essential to political order.[9] A unified system of law, not unified government, was what gave unity to the state, in his view. Bentham certainly preferred centralized and unified government, and he used its advantages in the way of efficiency and responsibility to attack mixed government. Indeed, the organization of unified government was of greater interest to him, and even perhaps of more importance for the responsible character of rule, than popular elections and the other apparatus of democratic representation. In addition, Bentham wrote as if unified government were a necessity because his command theory of law required a single, designable body whose "will" is expressed. Still, he admitted that whatever form it takes, unified government is only "commonly found," and is not absolutely necessary for order. Neither the immaturity of some governments nor the insignificance of some states turned solely, in his account, on its presence or absence (I, 103).

Despite Bentham's own preoccupation with the organization of unified government, his writings on democratic representation have received immeasurably more attention, and democratic representation too must be dissociated from popular sovereignty. *The Constitutional Code* contains Bentham's most doctrinaire argument for simple representative government; he advocated one popularly elected legislature, entirely without admixture of lords and crown. The happiness of the people can only be guaranteed protection by this form of government, he wrote there, and he called the people the "constitutive power." In this scheme, the people are electors. They choose and remove governors (IX, 10, 97, 155-157). Now, the entire course of Bentham's thoughts on representative democracy has been minutely mapped, and the task has proved difficult, above all because arriving at a political preference for one or another regime seems never to have been his chief object; only in *The Constitutional Code* is representative democracy set out plainly as just that—Bentham's political preference. But even if he did not always recommend unmixed representative democracy, Bentham seems to have recognized the close connection between utility and democratic values (including a broad, if not universal, franchise) from the start. The French Revolution inspired him to set out in something other than a casual fashion the relation between democratic principles and utility, though he addressed himself to the special circumstances of the French case.[10] *Plan of Parliamentary Reform in the Form of a Catechism,* written in 1809, plays a central part in every chronicle of Bentham's political preferences, because it contains all of the elements of radical reform: exclusion of placemen as voting members of the House of Commons, annual elections, universal and "practically equal" suffrage, secret ballots, and published records of House speeches. Still, the argument there is for "democratic ascendancy," not pure representative democracy (III, 457-461, 612-613), and Bentham admitted that his preference for annual parliaments and universal suffrage derived from their appearing more "defensible on principle" than deviations from these arrangements (III, 599). As its title suggests, the *Catechism* is a popular aid to faith, and faith is here, as ever, susceptible to doubt. Bentham was not confident that even universal suffrage would sufficiently diminish aristocratic influence on politics (III, 468n.), and the proposal he recommended most strongly in connection with electoral institutions was the secret ballot (III, 599-600). In fact, the one measure he argued for categorically throughout was publicity. The *Catechism* illustrates why it remains unclear whether and when Bentham became a committed democrat:[11] his principal arguments for democratic institutions were either speculative deductions from utility or preferences based on the estimate that popular elections appeared to be the least objectionable method of choosing governors.

Nonetheless, two points can be made with confidence about Bentham's thoughts on democracy. First, his argument for representative democracy turns on the view that popular elections are necessary if the self-interest of rulers is to be opposed; specifically, they are the best way to mitigate corruption of House members by the king's ministers.[12] Democratic elections are a form of self-defense, for Bentham (IX, 47). They are mainly negative. Parliamentary reform, he wrote in the Introduction he appended to the *Catechism,* is the "sole possible remedy against the otherwise mortal disease of misrule" (III, 435), and the medical metaphor indicates that the first object is relief. Radical reform is the alternative to national convulsion; it is not, by itself, health. The measures Bentham prescribed were designed to remove the worst obstacles to probity, intellectual aptitude, and active talent in governors. They were meant as antidotes to oppression and depradation.[13] They did not, by themselves, ensure good government. In fact, as far as the composition of the legislature was concerned, Bentham's claims for popular elections were modest. Elections might prevent the assembly from comprising a cabal guaranteed to sacrifice the general interest to its own particular interests (III, 617). What popular elections can do is ensure that the governors chosen are at least capable of securing the universal interest (III, 452); elections cannot ensure that they will actually do so. In short, the universal interest is only a unified one in the face of designable sinister interests, and popular elections are intended to avoid the worst conspiracy and favoritism (II, 248). The point of "practically equal" suffrage is not arithmetical equality, Bentham explained, but the absence of the degree of inequality that is the mark of deliberate partiality (III, 612). As for incidental corruption, it is, he acknowledged, simply unavoidable. Something more than the popular choice of governors is required for self-protection, though, even if we assume that the people choose men of the right character and class. For Bentham, the import of democratic representation was doubly negative, negative in both its object and the means to it.

In all of his writings on elections, Bentham insisted that the purpose elections serve owes more to the sanction provided by the possibility of loss of office than to the selection of governors (IX, 42). The punishment of removal is what restrains governors from misrule (IX, 151-152), he argued. Responsibility, and not the representative composition of government, was uppermost in his mind. He recognized further that popular sovereignty makes every official responsible to the people, not elected legislators only. Long before he proposed giving the "dislocative function" to the people in his *Constitutional Code,* he had recommended that judicial officials be subject to popular removal. This same power of removal ought to sanction every office, he wrote in the *Code,* including administrative ones (IX, 104-106). Where the people choose and, more important, remove governors, they have the most direct and effective form of self-defense against misrule. Of course, no institutional arrangement is sufficient for this; the people must be suspicious and vigilant in the performance of their self-protective functions. But not even suspicion can promise more than protection; it does not ensure good government, or utility, in practice.

A second, equally important observation follows from the negative character of democratic institutions. It is not surprising that Bentham gave some thought to forms of government and to democratic representation in particular. After all, in the late eighteenth century no political theorist could avoid these questions, and it is clear that Bentham did not invent most of the democratic reforms he espoused.[14] What is of note, in light of the common view of Bentham, is how little attention he gave to these matters. Bentham always stuck by his early remark in *A Fragment on Government* that democracy, the "government of all," is no government at all (I, 276-277). The question that interested him was precisely, "what is government?" It went beyond matters of government's form and composition, and extended to the particular activities of government officials. Representativeness, as a reflection of popular choice and even interests, is inadequate as a criterion for good government, Bentham admitted. None of the institutions connected with democratic elections and the composition of assemblies is adequate to explain or ensure good government—not the franchise, not annual parliaments, not secret ballots. Good government has to do with legislative and administrative processes—with the business of government, and what distinguishes Bentham's work is his study of the organization and reward of officialdom generally. His most original ideas pertain to the arrangements and procedures which ought to govern judicial, administrative, and parliamentary activities. He recognized as a matter of theory and gave institutional expression to the view that popular sovereignty makes every official responsible whether or not he is an elected deputy (IX, 62). Every political function is a delegation from the people (IX, 121). His interest, again, was in how officials act, that is, in how government ought to be arranged and in how rewards ought to be apportioned to ensure that officials act to give utility expression. Legislation is a matter of information and prediction, an affair of observation and calculation. The hearing given popular desires, which is necessary for this business, is not solely or adequately obtained by formal political representation. Even in *The Constitutional Code,* Bentham emphasized that a vote is not necessary to communicate knowledge and judgment (IX, 45); officials can and should influence legislation without having a vote in the assembly, for example. And, he continued, a vote in elections is not meant to communicate opinions on any particular political question or matter of law (II, 465; IX, 42). Information collection was one of Bentham's favorite themes. His recommendation of publicity was designed to inform the public of the doings of officials, of course, but also to inform governors of popular sentiments (II, 312). *The Constitutional Code* may be his most energetic argument for popular elections, but it is not mainly about that at all. Good government is its subject—how utilitarian legislation can be made practicable and what institutions are necessary to support it.

As the "constitutive power," the people distribute offices, but they do not create them. Their constitutive authority is not a constitution-making one. It is not a perpetual, creative power, but a limited official function, defined and given to the people by positive constitutional law, which is itself eminently changeable. Unlike popular sovereignty, the constitutive authority of the people is not a permanent or essential condition. For popular sovereignty implied, as sovereignty had implied historically, perpetuity of power as well as absolute and supreme power. Popular sovereignty is inalienable. Although Bentham did not distinguish perpetuity from inalienability in principle, his point was that popular sovereignty cannot be disrupted. Changes of government and legal reforms do not constitute a dissolution of the people's sovereignty. These are, from his standpoint, institutional changes that occur more or less in agreement with what utility would recommend. A political society, Bentham wrote, distinguishing it from patriarchal society based on temporary natural weakness, ought not to be incapable of continuing forever in virtue of the principles which gave it birth (I, 264n.). And this perpetuity is provided by his notion of popular sovereignty. It can exist altogether distinct from any institution—disembodied.[15] Ultimately, popular sovereignty is found in an attitude of vigilance and self-defense on the part of subject individuals.

Despite the precautions he took not to personify the state, and despite his care that the notion of popular sovereignty not obscure the individualist basis of political order, Bentham could not always resist applying the language of naturalism to the state and its institutions. He wrote, for example, of the "will" of elected assemblies (II, 330), but immediately explained that he used will in a figurative sense only, and demonstrated the majoritarian principle that lay behind it (II, 306). When it came to discussions of international affairs, Bentham did refer to the state itself as an independent sovereignty, and sometimes wrote as if the state were animated to defend itself and to maximize its power. This is not surprising. After all, the state was not just a set of practical institutions, for Bentham. It was the only possible order. And nowhere is this clearer than in his writings on the relations of states, as the next chapter explains. For now, suffice it to say that popular sovereignty was the idea Bentham used to explain power's origin in the desires (and obedience) of individuals, power's absolute character, and initiative and innovation as a necessary part of power's every exercise. Popular sovereignty is, in this view, entirely distinct from the sovereignty of Bentham's juridical formula, which is the subject of the next section.

Bentham's Command Theory of Law

The command theory of law is just that—a theory of law, and not sovereignty. "A law may be defined as an assemblage of signs declarative of a volition conceived or adopted by the *sovereign* in a state," Bentham wrote (*OLG*, p. 1). Command theory employs the term "sovereignty," but in a limited and purely formal sense. Where law is understood as a command, a unified "sovereign"—either an individual or a body—is quite simply a logical requirement. All laws are, then, "referrable *ultimately* to one common source" (*OLG*, pp. 9, 1, 54). Bentham's "logic of the will" took account of more than just laws; legislation is only part of the whole power of imperation, he explained, and imperation is only part of sovereignty (*OLG*, pp. 137-138, 81-82, 91-92). But the focus here is his definition of law, which is typical of command theory and typically formal: "Whatever is given for law by the person or persons recognised as possessing the power of making laws, is *law*" (I, 151n.).

Nothing in this was original, Bentham acknowledged, nor for that matter of very great interest (I, 151n.). The source of a law is only one of several respects in which it can be considered, he advised, even according to command theory. And Bentham never insisted that the sovereign source of a law is the most important thing about it. He resorted to the formalism of command theory in the interest of legal reform, and it is the use he put his formula to—the political values he hoped to serve by it and its emphasis on the validity of laws—that is important. In this regard, Bentham distinguished himself from later subscribers to command theory, who usually alleged that it was an entirely nonideological view of law, or one that simply valued order above all. It is a credit to Bentham that he made neither claim for his command theory. He never entirely separated it from matters of political preference or political reform. No one was more sensitive than he to the limited and practical purposes command theory was designed to serve; it was designed, he knew, to address the special question of the validity of laws. Its principal object was to establish a simple and efficacious system of validation, and Bentham understood what political values validation could and could not be made to support.

A theory of law which focuses on law's commanding source is designed to distinguish ruler from subject, Bentham knew. If command theory has as a logical requirement a designable sovereign, its political purpose is to point to designable subjects. Command theory is calculated, in short, to make the subjects of law aware of their subjectness. This is only partly accomplished by determining the sovereign source of law; it also relies on the law's force. The power of imperation is not self-sufficient. Therefore, insistence upon one sovereign source of law is connected in Bentham's work and in command theory generally with a second matter—the force of a law. The mandates of the master, father, husband, and guardian are as much the mandates of the sovereign as those of the general or judge, Bentham wrote, not because the sovereign directly specifies the individual acts in question, but because of "the general tenor" of the effects of these mandates. He meant by this their effectiveness, and explained that were the mandates of these authorities to meet with resistance, in all cases the business of enforcing them would rest ultimately with the sovereign. "Nor," Bentham added, "is there anything of fiction in all this" (*OLG,* pp. 22-23). He saw plainly that command theory's chief ideological purpose is to increase the efficacy of law, and he built force into his definition of law. The proposition that law is a declaration of the sovereign's will continues: "such volition trusting for its accomplishment to the expectation of certain events which it is intended should act as a motive upon those whose conduct is in question'' (*OLG,* p. 1). The force of laws can be increased in practice, Bentham proposed, if care is taken with their ''expression.'' The future tense is even more powerful for this purpose than the grammatical imperative, for by posing his will in the form of a prediction, the sovereign not only makes his volition known but also makes it palpable. He gives his subjects to understand that the motive he trusts to for producing the effect aimed at is of ''sufficient strength.'' The sovereign predicts that in spite of the subject's ''free agency,'' his command ''will be followed by obedience'' (*OLG,* p. 105).[16]

It is worth noting, however, that punishment is not the distinguishing feature of law for Bentham. Force is one respect in which law must be considered, but it does not characterize law. For example, common law serves the purposes of law, but it can be recognized as law *only* in respect of accompanying punishment, and this is simply an inadequate view of law, as Bentham saw it: ''It is evident enough that the mute sign, the act of punishment, which is all there is properly speaking of a customary law, can express nothing of itself to any who have not some other means of informing themselves of the occasion on which it was given.'' The act of hanging is no help in determining what acts constitute stealing; common law is like a blow to a dog (I, 227-228; *OLG,* p. 184).

Since it cannot be said that nonresistance was a value for Bentham under all circumstances, it may be asked why he subscribed to a view of law which aims at securing order by emphasizing the law's source and force, by emphasizing subjectness. Briefly, command theory characterizes law by its source and force in deliberate contrast to higher-law notions, and Bentham shared this opposition to higher law. Certainly, one of his purposes in working out a command theory was to emphasize the creative and innovative nature of law and to release legislators from the absolute constraints higher law commonly imposed on legislation. Still, Bentham often attacked higher law without appealing to a formal command theory of law. Moreover, unlike others who used command theory to oppose higher law, Bentham did not want to separate questions of validity and utility. According to Bentham's principle of utility, law and morals ''have the same center,'' and sanctions accompany both; indeed, law makes use of diverse sanctions, not punishment only. The distinction that was served above all by Bentham's attention to the formal source and force of law is the distinction between both law and morals, on the one hand, and advice and exhortation, on the other (*OLG,* pp. 14n.-15n.). Sanctions are instruments of social control, Bentham argued, and punishment does not have its own purposes. Punishment can have no effect—it cannot even be understood—without reference to the substantive laws which control it (*OLG,* pp. 141-142, 148). Punishment gives effect to moral and legal directives, and neither law nor morals aims at educating men. Sanctions act as motives; they do not change men's interests. Utilitarian legislation and the punishment it prescribes have nothing to do with character formation. All things considered, if Bentham promoted a command theory which emphasized a unified sovereign and the efficacy of commands, he was less concerned to prescribe the conditions of order or to advocate obedience than he was to clarify and delimit the character of political order. He had one additional object in view. By emphasizing commands, Bentham made legislation a constant and active business. In England, the judicial power has traditionally been the only active one, and the monarch and Parliament have merely controled its activities (II, 11). This situation he would reform, and his call for a unified sovereign was meant to contrast with the common-law system of judicial decisions case by case.

When Bentham insisted that there was "nothing of fiction" in what he had to say about the force of the sovereign's laws, he made a claim that distinguished his writings on command theory from those of others. He admitted that designable sovereigns do not everywhere exist (*OLG,* pp. 18n., 20n.). He was even less sanguine about the existence anywhere of the complete laws he thought might be produced once his logic of the will was grasped; not even a specimen of a complete law is to be found, he wrote (*OLG,* p. 183). Blackstone's view of natural law was based on the erroneous assumption that natural laws exist because they ought to exist, and that they ought to exist because a belief in natural law is necessary for order, Bentham explained. And he was not about to repeat this confusion of expositor and censor in the case of either sovereignty or expressions of the sovereign's will. Nor did he promise that where a unified sovereign issues commands to self-consciously subject subjects, legal order must result. Command theory promotes an awareness of subjectness which was always double-edged for Bentham; it could point just as well to the practicability of resistance as to the necessity of obedience. The complete and efficacious laws that command theory defines are, he knew, aspirations at best.

For Bentham, sovereignty was never the purely formal notion it is according to most command theory. Even in *Of Laws in General,* he tried not to obscure the political relationship the term "sovereignty" also connotes: "in point of fact (for to that point I still exclusively adhere) . . . ," he wrote, "sovereignty over any given individual is a matter which is liable to much diversity and continual fluctuation" (*OLG,* p. 20n.). The "efficient cause then of the power of the sovereign is neither more nor less than the disposition to obedience on the part of the people" (*OLG,* p. 18n.). The most important ingredient of efficacious laws is neither their validity nor their form, but the presence or absence of agreement about the values they serve—in short, political consensus. And Bentham advised that the force or efficacy of law may depend "in considerable degree on the existence, real or supposed, of some customs to which it is or pretends to be comformable" (*OLG,* p. 109). No formal view of law can create consensus; not even the principle of utility can generate agreement under all conditions. Of course, command theory is most likely to be appealing where there are disputes about authority and law, for promises of hierarchy and order are built into its definition of law. But Bentham never pretended to be able to define these contests out of existence. No formal theory of law can create sovereignty; nor did he argue that there ought to be obedience to some identifiable sovereign in every case. A question no command theory can tolerate was always in the forefront of his thought: "who is legislating and what is the relation between his interests and the greatest happiness?" Neither the source of laws nor their force had any meaning or value for Bentham apart from the relationship between the intention of the legislator and the disposition to obedience on the part of the people (*OLG,* p. 109). He did not attend in detail to what the conditions of political agreement might be. But he did use utility to urge that laws cannot be considered apart from their content —or, Bentham added, apart from the political processes by which they are administered.

The force of a law comes not only from its source in the sovereign, but also from the particular institutions that give it effect, and chief among these is the judicial establishment. The power of imperation, though supreme and unlimited, is not self-sufficient and complete, Bentham recognized (*OLG,* p. 137 and n.). The sovereign will is impotent and the sovereign's predictions are fake unless there is an accepted system of "adjective," or procedural, law. Consensus about the court system and, above all, accommodations made to the profession that operates it are principal conditions of law (III, 204). Bentham understood what many legal theorists have not—that not even the logic of commands can make law an independent system. Even where there is a designable sovereign, the outcome of his will depends upon the larger political circumstances within which he operates—especially, in Bentham's view, the legal profession.

It was one of his most important insights (and one he shared with Hobbes) that no one concerned with legal order can ignore the concerns and claims of the legal profession. This consideration inspired his writings on law, and none more than *Of Laws in General* and its command theory. Briefly, the efficacy of a system of law depends in large part on its ability to satisfy the need the legal profession has to rationalize its decisions by pointing to some existing norm.[17] Utility taken from this juristic point of view may be only one derivative view of utility, but it is an important one (*OLG,* p. 190). Validation is quite properly the profession's chief task. And this process under common law was a most unsettled one, Bentham argued (*OLG,* pp. 188, 189, 192). The record of common law—in truth nothing more than "scattered atoms"—contains only a partial and imperfect history of cases (*OLG,* pp. 185-188). It is not enough to substitute statutes for legal history, though. Statutes cannot serve the purposes of bench and bar without being patterned on some "idea of law"; statutes must be resolved into that idea to be understood (*OLG,* p. 12). Bentham's command theory was intended to meet lawyers' needs for determinate norms as nearly as possible;[18] that was his practical object in *Of Laws in General.* In short, he did not subscribe to command theory to satisfy his desire for order and obedience, so much as he used it as an instrument to control the legal profession.

Bentham's formal definition of law did not cause him to put political questions aside, then. No one was more aware than he that the validity of a law and its utility are separable, and that validity is not a substitute for utility. He did not insist that only laws conceived as the command theory prescribes can result in security. Common law can serve the purposes of law, he admitted; even particular autocratic acts may have something of the effect of general laws "in virtue of the more extensive interpretation which the people are disposed to put upon them" (*OLG,* pp. 152-153). In short, Bentham's command theory does not really address the question "what is law?" at all. Instead, as he tried to make plain, he spoke to the question "what is *a* law?" and directed his answer for practical purposes at the legal profession.

When he asked "what is a law?" Bentham recognized that the question was in the first instance a purely formal one—"abstraction being made of the propriety" (*OLG,* p. 308n.). The answer did not turn on the distinction between judicial decision and legislative statute. Nor was a law coincident with a statute; its integrity was logical, ideal, intellectual and not physical (I, 151n.). Bentham's "logic of the will" is most famous for requiring a unitary sovereign, but what he chose to emphasize about the logic of the will was that it could produce unified and complete laws, at least where conditions for legislation exist. The unity and completeness of a law about which he wrote so much had to do with the logical relations among different "aspects" the legislator could take toward an act. Bentham's point was that expressions of will, like statements, can stand in logical relation to one another. He proposed a logic according to which a given act would be commanded, prohibited, or left free (*OLG*, p. 173).[19] A law complete in expression, design, and connection would reflect one of these attitudes; it would entirely account for the sovereign's disposition of an offense (*OLG*, p. 157). The unity of a law lies in the fact that it marks out one offense, and because there is no limit to what constitutes an offense, the number of laws in a system is purely a matter of convenience (*OLG*, p. 170). Bentham proposed to clarify the status of actions by his logic and by his attention to the difficulties of making the dimensions of an act on paper square with the actual will (*OLG*, p. 127). That is why he emphasized law as an *expression* of the sovereign's will.

Bentham's logic of the will speaks directly to the courts and the legal profession (*OLG*, pp. 182-183) and takes into account their requirements. For all his attacks on lawyers, it is important that Bentham did not oppose the judicial ethos per se. One of the noblest characteristics of English tribunals, he wrote, is that they have "generally followed the declared will of the legislator with scrupulous fidelity, or have directed themselves as far as possible by previous judgments" (I, 326). He was a close observer of the costs the profession regularly inflicted by keeping to its business in this way; pain was often the consequence of *fiat justicia ruat coelum*. But in the common-law system *fiat justicia* does partial evil for the sake of the universal good, which consists in adherence to established rules (*OLG*, p. 195). Although in the common-law system the judicial ethos is unaccommodating, for precedent overcomes utility entirely, still, this ethos can be exploited to advantage where there is a complete system of law. Heaven may be preserved. The self-interested conservatism of the profession was, then, a value, in Bentham's eyes. Preoccupation with validation keeps lawyers from purely personal considerations of expedience; the judge who would otherwise burn whomever he wants is restrained by the recollection: "You had better not, it will be thought strange."[20]

This is not to suggest that Bentham was committed to the view that courts discover and execute, rather than make law. He wrote about the common-law method of deducing rules from other rules, "It seems as if it could not be right for a judge to prefer analogy to utility unless it were more easily agreed upon the former than the latter" (*OLG,* p. 107). Thus, neither his logic of the will nor his codification proposals would result in the elimination of judicial interpretation, or "judicial legislation." Bentham meant only to bring judicial interpretation to light and to control for it (*OLG,* p. 241). Where there is a complete code of laws, interpretation of the law's expression may not be necessary, nor will the question of the mutual relation of laws be left in doubt. But Bentham would not absolutely prohibit interpretation of the law's design. The judge still must ask what the legislator's will would have been if he had had the case at hand in view; the experience of the judge must correct for the lack of foresight of the legislator (*OLG,* p. 160). In the case of bankruptcy court, Bentham recommended judicial legislation outright so long as reasons accompanied decisions; this condition would ensure that decisions were remediable and that responsibility was fixed (V, 580). Bentham did not minimize what he was allowing. Interpretation is alteration; it extends or qualifies a law. It is, simply, always necessary (*OLG,* pp. 160-163, 239, 241; V, 579-580).

Conceding interpretation to the courts may be dangerous, but denying it is ruinous, Bentham cautioned. His work on command theory offered a palliative to these dangers; a complete remedy to the problem of interpretation is, once again, only an aspiration (*OLG,* pp. 239-240). Despite the emphasis command theory places on the ultimate and formal source of law, Bentham wanted the legal profession and legislators as well to face the fact that lawmaking and lawfinding are not absolutely distinct (*OLG,* p. 241). He knew that of all his reforms, this one flew in the face of the ideology of the profession. And even though he wanted to explode the myth that judges discover the law, he was not entirely insensitive to the reasons for it in the first place—quite apart from the sinister interests of the profession. The whole question of interpretation points after all to the dilemma of legalism per se, which is especially troubling in common law. The dilemma is that law must serve the dual purposes of security strictly understood and expedience. It is not a contradiction, but an insight into the critical problem of law, for Bentham to have accused common law of being at once too rigid and too unsettled; he understood what caused the legal profession's propensity to correct the inconveniences of legalism by leaning first to the side of *stare decisis* and then to the side of *salus respublica* (*OLG,* p. 191).

Bentham could not resolve this dilemma, which is inherent in every legal system and conception of law, but he could expose it. He could try to build the tension between *stare decisis* and *salus respublica* into the principle of legislation itself, and the delicate balance utility attempts is precisely between security of expectation and reform. But even together, social science and command theory's logical criteria cannot do away with legal science, Bentham knew. They must accommodate it. No system can escape juridical practice in practice. Legislation and adjudication will both incline sometimes to greater flexibility and sometimes to greater certainty; they must guard against these twin dangers. Bentham's famous charge that the power of lawyers is in the uncertainty of the law was leveled against the practitioners of common law in particular (X, 429), but it was not his only word on the subject. There will always be uncertainty in the law. The charge of "discretion," Bentham realized, is only leveled as a term of opprobrium when there is disagreement about the values the law is made to serve. What really constitutes arbitrary power in a judge, he wrote, is his freedom from any obligation to assign reasons for his decision and his freedom from public scrutiny (V, 556).

Bentham was much taken up, of course, with questions of legal procedure, and his suggestions for the reform of "adjective" law indicate that there he would tolerate a great deal of judicial discretion. In the field of evidence, he prescribed many departures from common-law rules in favor of discretion, and he attacked especially exclusionary rules of evidence. Indeed, his proposals would replace formal rules of evidence almost entirely with warnings to the judge to "be suspicious." Bentham's attitude of reserve toward formal procedure here is not inconsistent with his political thought generally, for he always advised that nothing in formal procedures is a guarantee against legal oppression, and he warned that there is much in judicial procedure in particular that inhibits truth-telling and truth-finding (VI, 10, 88, 97, 101). It was not only rules of evidence that Bentham would transform, though; he contemplated a systematic alternative to common-law procedure: a "domestic," or "natural," system. Bentham called the system domestic because one judge acts alone, like a father, in his "search after truth" (I, 558). Three things characterize his decision making: he is impartial, he need not abide by fixed rules or standards of procedure, and most important, there is no alleged wrong of which he can refuse to take cognizance (II, 46). That is, the judge must perceive grounds for the reconciliation or punishment of the contesting parties. Evidence is not used to fit facts to a rule, here, but to arrive at a decision from the facts, according to the principle of nondisappointment. The process is not unlike arbitration; it bears some similarity at least to free decision from case to case (II, 47; V, 522).[21] What natural or summary justice does is keep the notion of injury at the center of the administration of justice, and provide satisfaction to the injured. Bentham's inspiration here is not difficult to discern: the common law boasts that there is no right without a remedy, but it is equally true of common law that where there is no remedy there can be no right (I, 186-187). This he would correct.

Bentham did not mean to oppose legal values with these recommendations. He was aware that the purposes served by law are not always best served by formal rule following. And his domestic tribunal retains what he properly took to be the essence of judicial proceedings—a suit between parties; indeed, he emphasized this by his insistence on the parties' personal confrontation wherever practicable. Bentham based his suggestions too on an assumption of the judges' impartiality. And his concern was for the "truth of the case," which rested as it always had on the proof of facts (III, 198; I, 558; II, 47). Briefly, he subscribed wholeheartedly to the value that judicial proceedings consecrate above all others—the value of having a controversy decided. Judgments, he wrote succinctly, put a period to a cause (*OLG,* p. 223). The judge must afford "immediate relief" (III, 322). Judicialization from this point of view is the mark of several of his proposals for institutional reform, including Panopticon and his essay on parliamentary tactics. According to the latter plan, Parliament would have a president who epitomizes judicial power in its simplest form and under the best possible circumstances, for in his presence "complaint, judgment, execution" follow one another instantaneously (II, 330). This model of a natural system of justice, with its swift and responsible decision making, rather than Bentham's command theory of law, was bound to appeal to those who value order above all.

Nonetheless, the desire for order, for effective decisions, is not enough to guarantee it, Bentham knew. Institutional changes in the judicial establishment have no more meaning or value apart from a unified substantive legal system and the values it serves than do the formulae of command theory. Whether Bentham's subject was the command theory of law or the organization and operation of government, his purpose was to make utilitarian legislation possible. The principle of utility would provide laws with their content, but it remained to ask: "Who ought to legislate?" Bentham criticized the legal profession for having usurped legislative functions, but the empire of lawyers is perfectly comprehensible, indeed a necessity, he admitted, where legislators are apt to be un-lettered soldiers, narrow-minded priests, or an "interrupted, unwieldy, heterogeneous, unconnected multitude" (*OLG,* p. 240). Good govern-ment depends for its operation only in part on an attitude of suspicion on the part of the people; the notion of popular sovereignty was never far from Bentham's mind, but it was by no means his sole preoccupation. Modern institutions are required to support utilitarian legislation and, by their organization, to create responsible public servants, as Chapter 6 explains.

5. The Sovereign State

Every state regards itself as bound to afford to its own
subjects protection, so far as it is in its power. (II, 544)

Historically, sovereignty was part of the ideological apparatus of absolutism in an era when consolidation of the power of kings was the chief
political object. This consolidation was commonly resisted by clerics or
in the name of clericalism—by those, that is, who would continue to enforce the restraints imposed on rulers by articles of faith. Opposition focused on two matters: toleration at home and the free formation of alliances abroad. One mark of the consolidation of absolutism came, it is
generally agreed, when kings afforded one another recognition and
formed alliances for reasons that ceased to be governed by bonds of
faith; the determination of sovereignty was a matter for the king's peers
as much as for his subjects. From the start, then, one principal forum for
the exercise and proof of sovereignty was "external affairs," though the
phrase must be set off in quotations since this distinction between domestic and foreign affairs was itself the creature of sovereignty's success. The
political development of monarchical absolutism did not result immediately in the secularization of rule. Unity of religion was the instrument
kings used to homogenize and order the realm, and religion continued to
be the chief ground of resistance to kings. The result of the consolidation
of absolutism was, instead, the establishment of the parochial character
of kingly rule and of modern states. This parochialism was of a new sort,
distinguished from the ancient cultural parochialism of the Greeks, for
whom the rest of what we call mankind were barbarians, and distin-

99

guished too from the later parochialism of peoples or cultures for whom all other men are aliens or new barbarians. Modern parochialism entailed acknowledgment of the existence and common status of similar political entities; it was marked by the mutual recognition of kings, and then states.

Although Bentham clearly opposed the personal character of monarchical absolutism, he was an advocate of absolutism. He rejected any limits to the matters or measures that might come within the rulers' exercise of power, and he recommended the consolidation and centralization of power. For Bentham, a new ethical basis provided absolutism with its purpose; a new rationality—utility—stripped it of its caprice. Bentham was not satisfied that absolutism tempered by utility had been sufficiently realized, when he wrote. For one thing, until social psychology was understood and adopted by legislators, techniques for arriving at this new public rationality remained primitive. For another, until the institutions of government were modernized, utility could not be given expression in law. And there was still political resistance to absolutism in practice; it was not by accident that Bentham called the English legal profession a "tribe" opposed to modernization. However, one critical accompaniment of absolutism was realized: Bentham did not have to prepare his readers for the idea of the parochial state or, as he termed it, "municipal" government: "The fact of its being established is notorious and its necessity alike obvious and incontestible" (I, 101n.), he wrote. And he could assert with confidence that conflicts of law occur most frequently between superior and subordinate authorities in a state, rather than between laws made by "independent sovereignties, each moving within their sphere" (*OLG,* p. 131).[1]

Recognition of the "universal necessity" of municipal governments and of "independent sovereignties" does not necessarily mean that anything like the continental doctrine of reason of state is the accepted way of thinking about international affairs. Enlightenment intellectuals recognized states as a matter of practice, without adopting the point of view of reason of state. In their writings, they either ignored the relations of states, abandoning this entirely as the arena of pure power and inevitable irrationality, or they proposed ways to transcend this state of nature (the result of the egoism of states) and proselytized for a world state or federation which would usher in universal and perpetual peace. Bentham too characterized the relations of states by the absence of any superior power; he thus assigned a clear demarcation between internal and external affairs. But if international relations were unique—and he coined the term—he did not allow that their conduct was inevitably capricious. Just as the state was not a fact only but also a norm of order, for Bentham, the system of states too (as the phrase indicates) might have a particular order to it. It was this order Bentham explored, an order that, in his view, need not operate at the expense of the egoism or best interest of states. The consideration he proposed in order to achieve rational egoism in international affairs was the principle of the common and equal utility of states. He argued for it in his early manuscript *Principles of International Law,* and the principle was still adumbrated in his last major effort, *The Constitutional Code.*

Recognition of the common and equal utility of states had historical antecedents, and Bentham made reference to one. "Monarchs wage wars of rivalry and not emnity," he observed, and every monarch is to every other "an object of respect" (IX, 129). Similarly, it was characteristic of state theory from its inception that conduct in international relations was actually governed and even justified by the necessities of preservation and power. This was supposed to be admitted even by enemy states in times of conflict. For Bentham, of course, the respect due other states rested on their ethical basis in individualism and not, for example, on the identification of the king's interest with the whole. And the regard one state must have for another was not restricted to comprehending its drive to preservation, but seemed in his account to extend to the other's welfare more broadly. Still, the equal utility of states is essentially a matter of mutual recognition and regard. It does not require a philanthropic attitude toward other states, only a diplomatic one. The main point here is that Bentham's principle of the equal utility of states is quite different from Enlightenment cosmopolitanism, despite the tendency to interpret the principle of utility in international matters as if it required calculating the interests of all men.

Bentham was not ignorant of this other universalistic standpoint, and occasionally identified himself with it. But his principle of the equal utility of states substitutes for cosmopolitanism, and the considerations it requires are quite different. Nothing can make Bentham's acceptance of the state as a norm clearer than this principle. Rulers must take into account the utility of other states when their policies affect them. But neither rulers of states nor "cosmopolitan legislators" need consider the interest of the greatest number of men simply. It is the utility of other states that they must have regard for—of states regardless of their form of government. Indeed, Bentham deviated even further from the universalistic ideal because it is not all foreign political entities whose utility must be considered, but only the utility of states likely to be affected by conduct in international affairs. The illustrations accompanying the principle indicate that in his mind it was ordinarily restricted in its application to the regular and informed relations of the states of Europe.

A citizen of the world, in preparing an international code of law, would take as his object the "common and equal utility of all nations," Bentham proposed at the start of *Principles of International Law.* Would the duty of a particular legislator, acting for a particular nation, be the same? "That moderation, which would be a virtue in an individual acting for his own interests, would it become a vice, or treason, in a public man commissioned by a whole nation?" (II, 537-538). Here then, in somewhat altered form, is the question that inspired reason of state thinking. In the continental tradition of reason of state, the rules that governed the conduct of private men in Christendom were challenged by the new standard of necessity of state. Bentham, by contrast, juxtaposed two utilities: on the one hand, the principle of the equal utility of all states (a consideration that is presented tentatively as a luxury of the citizen of the world); on the other hand, utility simply (or rather, not simply), which recommends moderation to private men, and which compels rulers to care for the happiness of subjects under their direction.[2] Bentham answered his query in what first appears to be an enlightened spirit: it is the duty of a ruler of a particular state, as well as the duty of a citizen of the world to employ the principle of the common and equal utility of states. In the course of his argument, however, Bentham makes it clear that the chief and controlling reason for a ruler to consider the utility of other states is precisely that it is in the best interest of his own state and of the happiness of his subjects to do so. "In order to regulate his proceedings with regard to other nations, a given sovereign has no other means more adapted to attain his own particular end, than the setting before his eyes the general end" (II, 538). This is no mere rhetorical ploy by which Bentham hoped to gain the ear of diplomats for his principle of equal utility. It is its rationale. Consideration of the equal utility of states turns out to be a technique of reason of state—a technique by which the ruler can preserve and protect the interests of his own state in the face of challenges by other states and in the face of traditional moral constraints on policy.

In domestic affairs, popular sovereignty operates as a restriction on every exercise of power. In the course of his career, Bentham also observed, no legislator can fail to experience a certain resistance to his policies by other states. In seeking the line of least resistance, he must be guided by the utility of other states likely to be affected by his conduct.

Bentham wrote: "how small soever may be the regard which it may be wished that he should have for the common utility, it will not be the less necessary for him to understand it. In the first place, that he may follow this object in so far as his particular object is contained in it;—secondly, that he may frame "according to it, the expectations that he ought to entertain, the demands he ought to make upon other nations" (II, 538). Bentham was optimistic that attention to the utility of other states would disclose common interests, which men would otherwise overlook. His hope was always that matters of common utility would increase, indeed that universal and perpetual peace was possible. When he advised that no method was more sure by which a sovereign could attain his own end than to act as if he had no other object than the extended welfare of all nations, Bentham was not recommending deception (II, 538). This was no Machiavellian technique to hide egoistic policy behind ideal purpose. But neither was it an assumption that an actual harmony of interests prevailed. Bentham meant only that where common interests exist, a ruler can for simplicity substitute the larger interest for his own state's interest. This having been said, the indication it gave of certain shared interests was not the only recommendation Bentham made for the principle of the common and equal utility of states. His principle pointed to common, and equal, utility. In international conduct, impartial consideration of the utility of all states is necessary even where no common interest exists. Again, the calculations required by the principle are a technique for determining the line of least resistance to policy. These calculations are simply part of the rational pursuit of self-interest. The principle compels rulers to look to consequences. Briefly, nothing in Bentham's principle of international affairs denies full acceptance of state egoism.

The duty to consider the equal utility of all states obliges the state, first, to do no injury and to do the greatest good to other nations "saving the regard which is proper to its own well-being" (II, 538). This duty, Bentham allowed, does not go beyond what the best-interest-of-state doctrine recommends and what is regularly followed. Insofar as it demands something more—philanthropy—it is philanthropy within strict limits, as the reference to present practice makes clear. According to the inaugural declaration Bentham composed for rulers, they must pledge to perform good offices for the people and on their behalf for the rulers of other states, but not offices that go against the "rightly presumable inclination" of their fellow countrymen or actions that are at their expense (IX, 203). Philanthropy does not extend to self-sacrifice, then. And nothing in Bentham's principle points to ways in which the welfare of humanity must be actively served; it does not, for example, prescribe a policy of providing universal subsistence. The principle of equal utility requires in the second place that no state receive benefit or injury from other nations without taking account of the "regard due to the well-being of these same nations" (II, 538), and here the standard appears more likely to conflict with state egoism. But even in this case, no hidden sacrifice is implied. Bentham accepted the exigencies of preservation, that is, of adequate power, and he did not urge states to act at the expense of these. Security remained his chief value. He advised only that a state's position vis-à-vis other states may require it as a matter of policy to absorb injury or to abjure praise. Finally, the passage most difficult to reconcile with acceptance of state egoism is the one which urges all men to regard as a crime every proceeding by which a nation does more evil to foreign nations taken together (or to those nations whose interest might be affected by an action) than good to itself (II, 538). This recommendation does, however, permit some injury to others in the course of self-help. And the illustrations accompanying the dictate mitigate it further; seizing a port that is of no use except for an attack, or closing seas and rivers by force or fraud to impede commerce, are both opposed by Bentham precisely because they do not contribute to the "offender's" own wealth and security. His prescription is diluted even more by the admission that by their reciprocity injuries may compensate each other. He had no objection to wars aimed at collecting compensation for damages suffered (IX, 202).

Bentham did not resort to philanthropic arguments, then, and it remains to observe that neither did he appeal to traditional rules of morality in international affairs. "Do as you would be done by," a rule of gold for individuals, is a rule of glass for nations, he lamented (X, 206). Even so, he did not choose to advance the golden rule as a rule. Clearly, the standard of the common and equal utility of states is no golden rule; it turns on an estimation of consequences. Indeed, Bentham inverted the moral formula when he argued that prudence recommends reciprocity.

Although international harmony was conceivable, Bentham did not propose the principle of common and equal utility of states solely because it pointed the way to perpetual peace. His design was not to overcome state egoism but to rationalize it, even where conditions of common utility do not prevail. Where it does not indicate some common utility, the principle still provides a technique for arriving at the line of least resistance in international affairs. In short, it offers efficiency as a standard for estimating diplomatic conduct and looks to restrict the nature and range of injury. By itself, the principle does not give direction to foreign policy; it is rather an antidote to crude and capricious egoism. The principle of the equal utility of states is meant to mitigate the influence of personal animosity and national prejudice in foreign affairs. In practice, Bentham wrote, international relations are inspired not by interest, justice, or humanity, but by the temper and affections of sovereigns (X, 210). He would replace the personal sympathies and antipathies of rulers with interest, justice, and humanity; wherever the subject of international conduct arises, Bentham's language is just this mix of moral aspiration and prudence. They come together for him in the term he used to pose the question on which *Principles of International Law* turns—is "moderation" a virtue or vice in international affairs? It is moderation he would institute by his principle of equal utility, not bare prudence, but prudence ennobled by the ethical status of the state and made possible by the historical condition of the modern state.

For now, suffice it to say that Bentham's principle does not guarantee common utility, absence of conflict, or even avoidance of war. He acknowledged war as one way of exercising power. Though war is the worst evil on account of its "extent" (II, 539), Bentham never proscribed it.[3] War is a way of enforcing rights and obtaining satisfaction. Where no common tribunal exists, he advised, concessions to injustice invite fresh injustice, so there is something to be said for a nation's not conceding anything of what it looks upon as its rights (II, 552). War is a means of settling disputes; Bentham even called it a "procedure" (II, 539). He would legalize it, minimizing its evils through laws of war. His list of good-faith causes of war is very nearly exhaustive, and consistent with his purpose of rationalizing state egoism, he reduced *mala fides* to ambition, insolence, and malevolence (II, 539-540). Whether or not a state resorts to force should depend in part upon its relative strength and in part upon the state of mind in which the injury it received was dealt, Bentham explained (II, 545; IX, 202). Where a state is the object of malevolent injury, he recommended war even against a superior enemy (II, 545). Alternatively, he advised Sweden to sue for peace against a superior enemy. His reasoning was the same in these disparate cases—it rested on his estimate of how best to save the state and what remained of its arms. Preservation, Bentham wrote in this context, is liberty (X, 203). Preservation is a law of behavior for states, but its prescriptions differ for particular states.

He thought of war as an acceptable if not inevitable way of exercising power, then. And he did not disregard the requirements of preservation and well-being, of power. In fact, Bentham was especially interested in the organization and material equipment of military forces. He was convinced, it seems, that logistics had become the critical measure of military strength (IX, 333). Bentham contemplated the possibility of a mutual reduction of armaments, but he did not urge unilateral arms reduction and he did not proselytize for disarmament. Arms were not, in his view, a cause of war, and he represented the standing army as an advance of civilization (IX, 334, 337). Arms reduction was a goal chiefly because of the cost of mobilization; again, the standard Bentham applied was efficiency. The same standard of efficiency informs his remarks on the subject of alliances. He denied that they were absolutely necessary, and where unnecessary, they were worse than useless and actually decreased security; his recommendation that Britain not pursue a continental alliance was strategic: a matter of her "matchless strength." Still, prudence might enjoin and justice might authorize other nations to enter alliances (X, 207). In this view, power was an exigency imposed by all international conduct, and Bentham was concerned with its efficient exercise by states. When he wrote that Britain—with or without Ireland, but stripped of its other dependencies—had no reasonable ground to apprehend injury from any one nation on earth, he was not referring to actual conditions of international harmony, but to Britain's superior strength (II, 546). Philanthropy and the legalization of international affairs were ideas he directed at states whose existence was manifestly secure; he addressed himself, after all, to England and France. Equality, he knew, specifically the equal status accorded states by international law, is most likely to be promoted by the strong.

In Bentham's hands, the principle of the equal utility of states was a technique of reason of state. He accepted the egoism of states, not only as a fact but also as a norm of order. Certainly, he did not share the Enlightenment's characteristic longing for cosmopolitanism. Perhaps the best example of his deviation from Enlightenment ideas is the case Bentham made for ending colonial rule. He did employ the contemporary language of emancipation, and wrote of the "cause of humanity." He even appealed to the rights of man (II, 551; IV, 408), and this alone suggests the rhetorical strain of these passages. In a more concrete vein, Bentham criticized the sacrifice of colonial interests to those of the mother country (II, 548). But whether colonies suffered injuries was a purely empirical matter that varied from case to case, he admitted. And he did not ignore the advantages enjoyed by those subject to colonial rule (III, 53); he recommended emancipation principally for colonies settled by the mother country, not for natives (III, 52-53).[4] The point he emphasized was that governors cannot serve the interests of inhabitants of distant territories well (IX, 202), and this is an argument for the expediency of consolidated states as much as it is an argument against exploitation. Indeed, the question of exploitation was a secondary one in these writings, for the cause Bentham pleaded was not the colonists' cause so much as the cause of the citizens of the colonial power. He appealed to the French to abandon the "weak and vulgar" ambition of holding colonies and to embark on a new path of glory by emancipation (IV, 408). This can be interpreted as an effort to find a standard bearer for the universal principle of self-determination. But it is equally and in this instance better described as an appeal to self-interest. In particular, Bentham took pains to demonstrate the real cost of colonies to the mother country, and it is mainly from the point of view of cost and benefit that he opposed colonial rule. Colonies bring no surplus revenue, are unnecessary from the standpoint of markets, breed corruption at home in the form of peculation by ministers and colonial commissioners, and cost money to defend (IV, 410-411; III, 53-55; IV, 416). Even if colonials were to vote to continue dominion, he insisted, it should be denied them. He argued for emancipation on the grounds of the best interest of the state. And Bentham did not propound self-determination as a principle; where the security of British investments abroad requires it, he wrote, investment companies should appoint the local governor and retain a self-protective veto on all laws (II, 563; IV, 417).

Bentham's view of international law, too, is entirely consistent with his assumption that a system of states is the form political order must take and that states are characteristically egoistic. International law may moderate their behavior, but it does not overcome egoism. What it does above all is consecrate statehood as the norm of order and recognize that in foreign affairs relations are mainly, if not exclusively, relations between states. International law is law by metaphor only, he cautioned (III, 162), and Bentham was the first to admit that international law is an aspiration. These laws do not exist. They are not "there" unrealized, waiting to be discovered. The existence of a law of nations was an illusion held by the "legislating Grotii," who tried to do from his armchair what Alexander and Tamerlane did by traversing the globe, and who merely succeeded in fabricating "false laws in the simplicity of his heart" (III, 220). International law has not been, nor can it be, the product of a wise legislator or outsider. The only way to achieve unanimity in international affairs, which is what the traditional law of nations aimed at, is by force. The pope had sought a mathematical line which would end the war over discoveries forever, Bentham recalled by way of example, but this effort depended on the view that the earth was flat and on the fact that the "servant of servants was the ruler of kings." Now the power of the Triple Crown has been retrenched (II, 539-540n.). Bentham criticized England for pretending to step into the void and act as arbiter in world affairs; England imitated the pope, he wrote, and harbored the illusion of being the latest dispenser of justice (X, 210). This role was not only impracticable, but also self-deluding, for England's policy in Europe showed that it had become Defender of the "Breach" of Faith in practice (X, 203). Bentham's view of international law, by contrast, was that there are areas in which states have common interests and where rules can be drawn up to which they might agree. His favorite example was a modest one: Catherine II's law of prizes. He looked ahead to the legalization of state relations as far as possible and recommended, among others, laws pertaining to succession and boundaries, which would reduce the incidence of resort to violence. An international tribunal, he proposed further, would provide alternative means of settling disputes to war. International law did not promise to eliminate disagreement or violence; it was a palliative (II, 545). Again, what is most important here is that Bentham's effort to legalize the relations of states indicates as well as anything that the state was, for him, a norm or order, now to be consecrated in law.

The principle of the equal utility of states is meant to be an antidote to prejudice and amimosity. It cannot and is not designed to overcome state egoism. This has been obscured, in part, because of the inclination to interpret Bentham's principle of utility as if it required cosmopolitan considerations. Bentham's purpose has been obscured, too, by his loathing of political men and his criticism of their policies. The divergence of interest that he saw everywhere between rulers and ruled marked foreign policy as well, and Bentham tended to describe wars as wars between rulers. He spoke as if there were a universal alliance of peoples against rulers, disregarding for the moment his parochial political view of "people." Even so, his dissatisfaction with present foreign policy did not lead Bentham to imagine that democratic representation alone would put an end to war; the people are most often more warlike than their rulers, he admitted. Finally, his commitment to true reason of state is obscured by his reluctance to personify the state, for continental reason of state thinking turned on a view of the state as a living organism with a will. Bentham never relinquished his emphasis on the individualist basis of states, and he rarely succumbed to the language of naturalism. This meant that each state had, for him, its own particular requirements for preservation but not its own personality. He denied that the state has a "person"; "mists rise" when the state is spoken of in this way, he wrote. Simply, every state regards itself as bound to afford its subjects protection from injury by subjects or governments of other states. The utility of this disposition is evident, and its existence no less so (II, 544). Nonetheless, Bentham recognized that identifiable individuals and their interests are not always an adequate basis for discussing international affairs. Even if the state cannot be said to have a person, it does have interests apart from the particular ones of its citizens. A nation has its property, honor, and condition, all of which may be affected without the individuals who compose it being affected, Bentham conceded, though he did not enumerate them. The state has individualism as its basis, but it cannot be understood solely as a buffer from injury, which is how Hobbes described it.[5] For Bentham, the state comprises a higher rationality, or utility, to which subjects owe loyalty, and which requires their support.

Historically, the doctrine of reason of state has had two aspects. Theorists set out general exigencies which were said to govern the conduct of all rulers or states—preservation of the state and the maintenance of power were chief among these. At the same time, they offered specific admonitions to rulers, in response to the special circumstances of their rule. Bentham did both, as *Letters of Anti-Machiavel* shows. There, he reiterated the general necessity of attending to the common and equal utility of states, and at the same time, he criticized England's continental policy in particular. The tone of that work is suitably mixed; Bentham enjoyed the intellectual satisfaction of enunciating a general law meant to govern governors in affairs of state, and he showed off his diplomatic perspicacity. He clearly exulted in the conviction that he had taught Lord Lansdowne, expert in foreign affairs, something about the conduct of England's foreign policy, and he raged at the injustice he believed he and his brother suffered for having challenged the crown on this matter (X, 212). By their titles, however, both *Principles of International Law* and *Anti-Machiavel* announce themselves as antithetical to reason of state thinking, at least when it is understood as pure Machiavellism. This is not surprising in an author of the Enlightenment tradition, although it is worth noting that titles alone are not decisive, and that Bentham would not have been the first to accept reason of state under the protective title *Anti-Machiavel*. Bentham's work was neither camouflage nor casuistry, though; his was a genuine attempt to accommodate the two traditions.

He was confident he could recognize Machiavellism when he saw it—

secrecy and hypocrisy were its marks. Machiavellism was triumphant in international affairs, Bentham wrote, where "to do mischief is honour: to do it slily, darkly, and securely, is policy" (X, 206). Most men think there is more pride in being accounted strong than resentment at the title "unjust," he observed, and the imputation of injustice is flattering where the state is at stake (II, 552). Crimes in pursuit of individual interest, it was commonly said, are virtues when performed on behalf of national interest (II, 556). Bentham was quite frank about the appeal Machiavellism had for him; even as I write, he admitted, the sentiment is still dear to my heart. Bentham meant to attack not only the mischief of Machiavellism—above all, deception[6]—but also the idea that there is honor in it. He warned that this peculiar sort of prestige is bought at the cost of real strength. His object was to show the inexpedience of what he took to be the essence of Machiavellism, and to moderate the evil done in the course of pursuing the state's best interest. From one standpoint, Bentham's thought was coincident with reason of state, for he shared Machiavellism's concern with consequences and efficiency. There is nothing in his discussion of alliance policy, for example, that argues categorically against a breach of alliance; there is no principle in Bentham's thought he could invoke for such a prohibition. His criticism in *Anti-Machiavel* is that British diplomats maneuvered secretly and unnecessarily to provoke breaches of alliances; folly and passion governed them, not interest. The continental policy was, he wrote, at once "impolitic and unjust" (X, 207). The moderation his principle recommends, his rejection of many of the traditional techniques of Machiavellism, is possible, as Bentham explained it, not so much where moral education and exhortation have done their work, as where certain historical conditions prevail. These conditions account for Bentham's ability to draw Enlightenment causes such as publicity and the cause of reason of state closer together and to make moderation (not cosmopolitanism) practicable.

Three assumptions underlie Bentham's principle of equal utility as a technique of reason of state. They indicate that the moderate character of his principle is, in part at least, contingent upon historical circumstances. The first assumption he made is that the chief purpose of reason of state is the preservation of established states. Bentham could emphasize institutional reform throughout his writings only because the existence of states was axiomatic. Reason of state thinking had not always recommended preservation simply, however. The doctrine was originally applied to the founding or regeneration of states, and it was commonly addressed to aspiring rulers. Machiavellism was necessary to counter resistance to the consolidation of territory and power. But when Bentham wrote, he was able to accept the consolidated state as a given. The great work of carving territorial states and centralizing power had largely been accomplished, he believed. The worst techniques, once useful in overcoming resistance at home or abroad, could be abandoned. In this context, Bentham emphasized one matter above all: moderation is possible where consolidation is the norm because conquest is then no longer a principal goal of states. Bentham characterized war as a means of settling disputes, a "procedure," and not as conquest. And he was aware that this development was a relatively recent one. Territorial acquisition only now ceases to be an ambition, he noted; conquest is a "madness" that does not belong to our age (II, 551). No action to annex another state's territory—no claim by England against even its arch-enemy France, to use his example—would be tolerated. Parliament would not grant the funds for such an undertaking even if effortless success were a certainty (II, 551). Bentham's hope was to put a stop to colonial acquisition as well (II, 556-557). The best interest of states argues against colonies, he insisted, and one reason is that war may be required to defend them. Colonies increase the vulnerability of the state, rather than add to its strength; they are "unnatural excrescences" on the natural body, he wrote (IV, 414). The metaphor shows plainly that Bentham's limited account of war's purposes is not owing to fear of great powers, and is due only in part to despair of rulers and to the need to restrain vulgar ambitions. The passage shows too that it is the cost of distant territories, not national self-determination, which inspired his criticism of colonialism (IV, 408). (America, he wrote, is "peopled with men of the English race, bred up in English habits," III, 612). The main point is that, for Bentham, moderation is inherent in the norm of the consolidated state.[7]

A second assumption helps account both for moderation and for equal utility as a principle in international conduct. Established states were understood by Bentham to constitute a system of states. Policy making requires "full knowledge of all circumstances," he wrote, if the consequences of conduct are to be calculated, and foremost among these circumstances is how the utility of other states is likely to be affected. As Bentham explained it, the principle of equal utility is a technique of reason of state to the extent that states act in a system where they mutually affect one another and where regular and informed relations make their interests calculable. The chief import of the principle of equal utility is that reason of state points not to national interest narrowly understood, but to what Bentham was the first to characterize as the international character of foreign affairs. Utilitarianism is not identical with cosmopolitanism, or with individualism universally applied. But neither is it pure parochialism. Utility recommends, in short, the true diplomatic point of view. Just as in traditional reason of state thinking, the restraint Bentham's principle imposes on rulers is said to operate with the inexorability of natural law; it is as necessary to consider the utility of other states if one is to obtain one's object, Bentham wrote, as it is necessary for a satellite approaching the sun to follow the course of the planet (II, 538). Bentham's recommendation (the one shared by Enlightenment thinkers generally)—to abandon secrecy in international affairs—appears from this standpoint as something other than faith in publicity as an instrument of universal peace. One reason for publicity is utilitarian from a purely parochial point of view; it restrains ministers who would otherwise act against the interest of their subjects by means of secret negotiations and treaties. Parliament's control of funds is an inadequate check on policy, Bentham warned, once the enemy is at the door (II, 555). But he also argued for publicity on other, international grounds, quite distinct from Enlightenment reasoning. A policy which depends upon concealment for its success is a vulnerable one, because "its successes hang upon a hair" (X, 205). This was always true, but now more than ever, for now the "eyes of Europe" follow every political move (X, 201). Bentham's recommendation of publicity was not purely moralistic, then: it was a response both to the increased power of European public opinion and to the well-informed state of European relations, that is, to the diplomatic and spy network in which Bentham took some interest. Secrecy is no longer expedient.

Historically, the institutional expression both of state egoism and independence (III, 584n.) and of the restraint imposed on international conduct by a state system is the idea of a balance of power. The balance of power assumes established states with regular relations and with a common interest in pursuing the "lines of least resistance." Bentham, at least, took it in this conservative sense. The balance of power was not, for him, based on the desire for a breathing space before expansion. It should be understood instead, he wrote, as a "point of repose in which all the forces find their equilibrium"—ideally an equilibrium difficult to depart from (II, 538). Balance in a constitutional system represented stagnation and death for Bentham, but not here; rest is the absence of coercion, the fruit of "mutual and universal independence" (II, 447). He was aware, of course, that this promise is entirely conservative from the point of view of a radical ideologist, for he admitted that no special constitutional structure is encouraged or guaranteed by the balance of power (IV, 410). And it is consevative in another sense, for a balance of power preserves the present inequality of states. Bentham did expect that poor and weak states would be kept from annihilation by this means (X, 202), but he never promoted the equality of states at the expense of security. In neither civil nor international affairs was equality a principal value for Bentham. He always viewed it negatively, in terms of reducing inequality for the sake of greater security. He acknowledged, therefore, that too much inequality between states is a cause of war in a balance of power system, but he was less concerned to increase the status of small and weak states than he was to prevent hegemony by the strong. In *Anti-Machiavel* he criticized England for treating the present balance of power as an arena for manipulating weaker states—he criticized England precisely for wanting to increase its already "matchless strength." There is a "point in the scale of national security, beyond which the nature of things will not suffer men to soar," he warned. "No step we can take can raise us above it," and "no effort we can make, but must endanger our sinking below it" (X, 207). Although prudence may recommend alliances for some states (X, 207), for England a continental alliance was a liability; fear, he wrote, is not favorable to security (II, 559).

Bentham accepted a state system which operated according to a balance of power, then, but he objected to the "vulgar commonplace mode of arguing on these subjects" (X, 208). He objected, that is, to a purely mechanical view of balancing. Automaticity is the result of traditional calculations of position based on military estimates. The best example of this, he thought, was England's automatic and senseless policy toward Russia (X, 203-206). No purely mechanical balance can ensure equilibrium, he judged, for it is too easily upset by wars of position. He challenged in particular the axiom that any increase of power by another state must be countered. He warned against implications of design and threat where there is no assignable cause. He recognized the danger that lies in exaggerating the dangers of great powers. The principle of the common and equal utility of states is negative; it serves as an antidote to the automaticity that often accompanies a balance of power. It reminds rulers of the possibility of common interests. It also suggests the possibility that interest and intention may diverge (IV, 417); men have too great a tendency to disregard the reasons others have to be just, he wrote, because they are so sensitive to their own deviations from right (II, 553).

113

Above all, the principle of equal utility mitigates automaticity by pointing to what Bentham thought of as real interests, rather than national prejudices and animosities.

The state system does not operate exclusively according to military estimates, he explained. Certainly, it does not operate in the traditional fashion, where ostentation was proof of power. Ostentation is bought at the expense of true strength, of wealth, Bentham argued. It is no longer possible to use ostentation to conceal the limits of wealth,[8] and he criticized Frederick the Great for pursuing opulence at the expense of the wealth of his subjects (III, 44n.). Bentham enlarged upon the present basis of power because the best interest of states demands more than anything else an understanding of what constitutes strength (II, 559). Briefly, it is from the point of view of economic well-being that Bentham opposed "vulgar" estimates of power and position. He questioned, for example, the economic rationale behind British policy to weaken the influence of France in Turkey (X, 211). The state system is based on regular and informed relations, he thought, chief of which is trade, and by emphasizing trade relations Bentham clearly hoped to rationalize state egoism. Splendor, greatness, and glory are incompatible with opulence, he wrote (II, 559-560). Traditionally, fictitious honor and dignity were bought at the expense of justice, probity, and effective benevolence, and at the expense of self-regarding prudence as well (IX, 201, 210). Bentham did not make the further argument that the interdependence of states which results from trade necessarily produces cooperation; it is clear that competition is equally likely to follow. But this sort of competition is bound to be more moderate than contests for prestige based on ostentation, Bentham judged; and it is certainly more moderate than dynastic and religious quarrels. He emphasized one moderating factor in particular, of course, the negative relation he hoped to demonstrate between colonies and wealth. Again, advantages in trade are not gotten from conquest or from the acquisition of colonies. Belief in the profitability of colonies is "modern alchemy" (III, 53). Colonies do not provide surplus revenue, and they are not necessary in order to establish markets (IV, 410-411; III, 53-54). If the luxuries they bring constitute profit for some men, they burden the rest (III, 52-53; IV, 412). There is, finally, the cost of their defense (III, 55). Two points stand out in these discussions. One is that when he wrote about trade here, it was the effect of trade on relations between states that Bentham had in mind. He did not expect economics to supersede politics. Trade depended upon the existence and intercourse of states, in his view; he did not consider trade from the standpoint of the relations of individuals or corporations. The other, related point is that his concern was for national wealth and for state security. The result of his principle would be to increase the chances of universal and perpetual peace, but these would only come from the strength of states, not their weakness or elimination.[9]

Bentham argued that most often prestige, ostentation, and even arms are bought at the expense of real strength, and that the burden for these excesses is borne by the people. The principle of equal utility could ensure more rational foreign policy. It could also serve the cause of order at home, he thought. For there is now a clear relation between the cost of power based on arms and war and the happiness of subjects. The relation between arms and war on the one hand, and taxation on the other has become clear. And it is equally evident that political stability turns in part at least on this matter of taxation. Thus, the third assumption which underlies the possibility of moderation in international affairs, for Bentham, is the importance of public opinion in politics (X, 204). Reason of state thinking was always concerned with the security and effectiveness of rulers, and the play of domestic interests was seen to operate as a constraint on policy abroad. Now, Bentham believed, regardless of the formal character of the regime, a truly public opinion acted to circumscribe ministers, as his notion of popular sovereignty shows. This is not to say that he thought public opinion would be a moderating force on policy in every case. For the last hundred years the people of England have forced their ministers to war, he admitted (II, 559; X, 204). They are jealous of their public men and at the same time diffident of them for being of the same mold as themselves; as a result, they dread being duped by others and are especially aggressive (II, 553). Public opinion, he insisted in a more optimistic vein, is educable; its prejudices can be overcome (II, 553). But the chief hope for public opinion as a restraint in international affairs comes from the fact that it instigates only short wars. The public acts from hatred, and hatred cannot be lasting when it lives at the expense of those who harbor it; policies which must overcome love of self are not likely to be pursued for long by a majority (IX, 32). Wars of rapacity, which were rational for the ancients, and even for modern despots, are not at all profitable from the point of view of the people who pay for them, Bentham pointed out. Conquest has no appeal to those who do not share in the plunder (II, 557, 551, 553).

There remains this to say about public opinion and its relation to reason of state in international affairs. Nothing in Bentham's recommendations for moderation or in his principle of equal utility rejects reason

115

of state thinking. If equal utility seeks the line of least resistance to the state's interests, it seems to permit all that is necessary in securing these interests. What is new here, and what distinguished Bentham most clearly from the continental tradition of reason of state, is that public necessity appears in his work as a genuinely public—manifest—necessity. Reason of state is not for him a mystery of statecraft. Bentham did not try to spare the public conscience. The domestic costs of security are clear, and so are the injuries likely to be inflicted on others during its pursuit. The principle of the equal utility of states does not guarantee the existence of common utility among states, although harmony is conceivable. Strict justice to other states requires conduct that is not partial, that is, not malevolent or based on anything other than diplomatic considerations. But neither the equality of states nor the equal welfare of their inhabitants is an imperative. The principle of equal utility does not require philanthropy toward other states or self-sacrifice. The standard it points to for foreign policy is efficiency. It looks to minimize evil. And it advises the public generally to accept this standard.

One conclusion above all follows from Bentham's writings on international affairs, and it cannot be emphasized enough. As concerned as he was with the happiness of individuals, and as desirous as he was to establish the ethical basis of the state in individualism, when it came to international relations, the happiness of men individually and universally was a derivative consideration. An increase in the happiness of all men may be the consequence of the state system he described, but care for the general welfare was not a principle of action. The actions taken into account by the principle of common and equal utility were the actions of states with regard to other states; Bentham was not concerned at all with the private activities of individuals or with the attachments and obligations that derived from common humanity. Men were seen, and quite properly in his view, as citizens or inhabitants of states. Where the state is a norm of order, as it was for Bentham, the care of men is a matter for their own state, and neither private individuals nor governors are constrained by utility to attend to men universally. The principle of the common and equal utility of states proposed by Bentham simply does not enjoin men to promote the security, equality, abundance, or even subsistence of all men. Humanity must be served, insofar as it is served directly at all, through the medium of states. To the extent that equality is a value, it applies to the independent status common to states, and not to the security or welfare of their inhabitants. And even so, it is clear that the strict equality of states was not an aspiration for Bentham. The equal utility of states that he spoke of had to do with impartiality above all. It meant that governors must consider policy without regard to the personality of rulers or to dynastic or religious considerations. At most, the principle of equal utility points to the preservation of established states. In short, the principle brooked no interference in another state's domestic affairs, not even for the sake of its people's happiness. The state as a norm inspires concern for the mutual and universal preservation and independence of states.

And this is true precisely because the state is a norm of order. It was the only conceivable sort of order, for Bentham, and he was certain that individuals would benefit by it. He had in mind economic advantages, of course, but the chief point here is that where states exist and foreign relations are governed by the best interest of states, the greatest chance for peace exists. It is clear why Bentham thought that peace is served if the state is the norm of order, and his reasons are, once again, negative. State relations governed by utility are diplomatic ones, and not fanatic. Common and equal utility is an antidote to the worst personal animosities and dynastic and religious quarrels. States do act self-interestedly, free of the traditional constraints imposed by dynastic ties and religious scruples. But they also act without the enthusiasm attached to these. And the relations of states according to the principle of common and equal utility avoid the worst sorts of ideological conflict. If the principle does not require philanthropy, neither does it require agreement about political preferences. The only political value that is universalized in Bentham's scheme is the value of the state itself, or of utility as its higher rationality (II, 502). He rejected outright the notion that any state has a real interest in guaranteeing the constitutional structure of any other (II, 549). The guaranteeing system, he asserted, is an abomination (IV, 410) and tyrannical (II, 549). Recognition or not of some newly formed government ought not to be a *casus belli*, he wrote in a similar vein (II, 545). Bentham valued constitutionalism and the institutional expressions of popular self-defense, including democratic representation, but in his view, these did not supersede reason of state and the value of states themselves quite apart from their form of government.

This having been said, it remains true that Bentham was most interested not in the state as an independent actor in international affairs, but in the state as a legal entity. The expression of utility, he repeated over and over, is a unified system of law. He was dedicated above all to a study of the institutions necessary to support the state as a legal entity, and this bureaucratic apparatus is the subject of Chapter 6.

6. Responsible Public Service

When the proportion between reward and service . . . is
our object, we must always consider of what nature the
service is, and what sort of men they are, who are to
perform it. *Burke, Speech on Economical Reform* (V,
293)

The main idea in Bentham's political thought is that a unified system of
law is the expression of the higher rationality he called utility. His writings were dedicated to explaining what makes utilitarian legislation possible and to investigating what institutions are necessary to support the
modern state conceived in this way as a single legal entity. Bentham ap-
proached the question of the state's institutional support from two sides.
He gave considerable attention to the organization of government, by
which he meant not only the formal character of the regime, but also the
organization of judicial and administrative establishments. In fact, these
permanent establishments interested him more than anything else about
government, for they are, he explained, the main supports of the legal
system. Their officials give effect to laws, and in the course of this work,
they study how laws should be modified and what laws should be added
or eliminated to accord with the legislators' intentions. Utilitarian legislation is, for Bentham, a continual process that does not begin and end
with the statutory expression of a sovereign's will. His *Constitutional
Code* focuses on organizing and managing a centralized (IX, 121) and
hierarchical (IX, 62, 204, 226, 229) officialdom, and this detailed scheme
looks forward to Weber's work on bureaucracy. In particular, Bentham
was concerned to organize officialdom in such a way as to maximize the
collection and communication of information useful for legislation; he
emphasized to an unusual degree officialdom's "statistical function"
(IX, 232-264).[1]

Bentham did not restrict his study of state institutions to organizational matters, however. Hierarchy, centralization, and rationalized rewards and punishments can make officialdom responsible, and that was his object—but only once responsibility is understood. Public service takes on a new meaning with his view of law and the state, Bentham thought, and all of the traditional ways of thinking about office only impede the modernization of government institutions. Office can no longer be understood as the property of a class. Officialdom cannot operate according to an ethos of benevolence, heroism, or virtue. Officialdom must have its own professional ethos, consistent with responsible public service, as this chapter explains.

Henry Brougham wrote essays honoring the statesmen he believed were mankind's true benefactors.[2] In contrast to his friend's purpose, Bentham's object invariably seemed less generous; as his own essay on Brougham proves, he was most concerned to strip the title of benefactor from the undeserving (V, 549). Bentham did not attend single-mindedly to measures, then. Few of his writings are free of the "passion and ill-humor" that arise when men are discussed (I, 231). To cite but one example, he deliberately set out to cause Peel and Eldon uneasiness with the papers he wrote about them (V, 279-280). Even so, Bentham's grievances were not purely personal. He wanted to reconsider the whole idea of benefactors. And because he thought that the greatest gift to a people is a utilitarian code of law, it is not surprising that his examination of the present lists of benefactors left their ranks practically bare. He struck from these lists England's lawyers and aristocratic officials, who respectively abused and neglected their parts in legislation. Good laws are possible only where lawmakers—that is, parliamentarians and judicial and administrative functionaries, who together constitute officialdom—understand what it means to describe legislation as a public service and to describe public servants as responsible.

Bentham's attacks on lawyers and aristocratic officials are reviewed in the first two sections below. All of his writings contain at least a few incidental animadversions aimed at lawyers and high officials, but one work, *Official Aptitude Maximized, Expense Minimized,* takes for its special subject a critical view of these two fraternities. *Official Aptitude Maximised* comprises eleven papers, and includes essays Bentham wrote in response to speeches by Burke, Rose, Peel, and Eldon. These pieces merit special attention. They represent Bentham at his rhetorical best. And they must have commended themselves to their author, for he took the unusual step of printing several of them more than once.[3] It does not need recapitulation of the work done by many eminent historians in the field of English political development to suggest that Bentham's arguments were of practical interest and import.[4] The papers show that Bentham's sustained assault on the brotherhood of lawyers and on aristocratic officialdom was not exhausted by the common charge of corruption. Lawyers and their aristocratic allies actively opposed the modernization of political institutions, he argued; the *esprit de corps* of both fraternities was incompatible with the ethos he thought ought to govern public officialdom. From his criticism of lawyers and the aristocracy came Bentham's alternative understanding of public service.

By public service Bentham referred in the first instance to the diverse concrete activities that make up legislation, specifically legislation which contributes to the happiness of individuals in the state. But wherever he wrote about public service, he gave equal emphasis to service's other side—its effect on the performer—and Bentham never lost interest in the question of how best to reward officials (II, 230). Public service has nothing to do with altruism, he insisted; legislation is not really a gift to a people at all. He took up, then, one of the great problems of state theory: the relation between common egoism and idealism. The satisfaction of rulers is part of utility, he advised. To do good for others at the expense of self-sacrifice, he wrote in another context, cannot be called governing at all (II, 548). The relation between service and its reward was critical for Bentham because by this relation governors are made responsible. Thus, for his discussion of responsible public service, Bentham chose a model which pointed at the same time to service's effects on the recipient and its effects on the performer. His model for public service was professionalism.

Bentham knew that professional services were only one of many kinds of services; indeed, he conceived of social intercourse as a whole as the mutual exchange of services. The care parents take of children (the "original" service) and acts of benevolence were alternatives to professionalism as a model for officialdom (I, 338; III, 179). What parental care and benevolence share with professionalism is that in every case the services performed are indefinite, and this character of indefiniteness also distinguishes professional services from all of those private services that make up the ordinary business of economic life. But professionalism, and not parental care or benevolence, was Bentham's model because the latter are inspired by purely personal sentiments for certain individuals. Public services, like professional ones, must be rendered impersonally and extend to men generally. In this respect, benevolence figured as a special case; even though psychology teaches that benevolent actions are not truly disinterested, there are instances where acts contradict all of the ordinary standards of prudence. It is possible for benevolence to extend beyond the usual circle of one's own to the public generally, Bentham conceded. But such a sentiment is rare,[5] and opportunities for men to perform extraordinary acts of benevolence are rarer still (II, 231); their coincidence is "accidental heroism." Bentham accounted for public services quite differently; while not always matters of routine, they are in most cases the outcome of a steady course of daily actions. Public services result from habitual occupation. Bentham insisted that habitual occupation, rather than any special personal quality, is what produces public services. He used professionalism to show that men do not need to recognize, rely upon, or educate other men for virtue in order that care be taken of the general happiness. Business, including the public business, can get on without any notion of character.

For Bentham, professionalism was an assurance of competence, which is demonstrated in the performance of some service. Standards are set and ultimately upheld by the fraternity, but the professional internalizes these; and public officials too ought to be in the habit of considering their conduct exposed to scrutiny, he recommended. It was the professional ethos that Bentham had in mind when he wrote of public service, and not formal training or validation. He advised that professionals make the best parliament men: an individual's capacity for office is always a matter of conjecture, he wrote, but "the best founded opinions are drawn from his habits of life, his attachment to his profession, and above all, the confidence reposed in him by those who are engaged in the same profession" (II, 195). Bentham was convinced, further, that he knew what underlies the professional ethos—what ensures professional behavior. A profession is a habitual occupation because it is regularly rewarded, and with the proper mix of money and esteem. Professional service, unlike virtue, is not its own reward. In the case of both alternative models for public service—parental care and benevolence—no regular relation between service and reward can exist. The occasions for these services and their content are entirely limitless. They are bounded only by the sentiments of parents or friends, for there is no end to the care of children or aid to neighbors. These services are rendered freely, spontaneously, and the reward in each case is internal. In short, benevolence is irresponsible. The only external reward appropriate to either one is gratitude, and gratitude can be neither proportioned nor compelled. In the professions, however, benevolent actions are performed self-consciously

121

and self-interestedly, and reward makes them regular. By appealing to professionalism as his model for public service, Bentham found a substitute for paternalism and, more important, for character in the modern state, as the third section below explains.

He was not unaware of the fact that professionalism and public service could conflict, and perhaps the first serious concern over the relation between expertise and public opinion is found in Bentham's writings. Intellectual dominion as a form of political aggression was a common theme in eighteenth-century political thought, but Bentham did not rest with attacks on the clergy. He attacked lawyers too, and not just as one group or class with separate interests, but as a profession specifically. The legal fraternity epitomized the dangers of professionalism; its *esprit de corps,* he wrote, is antisocial (II, 368). Not surprisingly, then, it was the other classical profession, medicine, that he turned to most often for his model of public service (II, 212). His object was to show that a public service with its own *esprit de corps* of responsibility was possible.

The Legal Profession

Bentham's attacks on the legal profession occasioned much of his fame during his lifetime, and he is still known for his denunciation of lawyers. Lawyers claimed his attention because, acting through the courts, they were the makers of English law. Contrary to the common view, however, they are not England's true benefactors, he wrote, and are not entitled to the respect they enjoy (III, 326). They make law but do not perform a public service. Moreover, the professional services lawyers do perform and for which they are rewarded have consequences that are demonstrably public disservices.

Lawyers do not perform a public service when they make common law above all because, they do not legislate publicly. They camouflage their legislative activity. The law, they claim, is "there": they only discover it in particular cases by following precedent, or the line of authority already set out. It is not their own reason but the "reason of the law" that speaks when a decision is pronounced, and this reason is inaccessible to the unlearned reader. In this way, Bentham argued, lawyers enjoy a peculiar irresponsibility. Their claim to be independent of any outside judgment is acceptable because they claim at the same time that they are not actually independent; that is, they claim not to make political decisions or to voice personal opinions but to subject themselves to some higher authority. This claim is typical of professionals, and Bentham did not expect even responsible officials to be entirely unlike professionals in this regard. But in the case of the legal fraternity in a common-law system it was a dangerous, to say nothing of hypocritical, claim. Even if precedent is closely followed, the only proper higher authority in the field of law is the principle of utility. There is no substitute for entertaining direct questions of utility, Bentham insisted. Besides, not even the cause of continuity is served by common law, for it is simply untrue that precedent is more easily determined than utility.

Bentham did admit that it was not unusual for the content of common law to coincide in practice with what utility would require: precedent and *de bonum publica* do not always conflict. Even so, he attached great importance to the claim that lawyers do not make law. And his reasons are plain. For one thing, if legislators are not identifiable in practice, they cannot be rewarded for actual services, and only a system of rewards can reduce the distance between prudence and benevolence and make utilitarian legislation dependable instead of occasional. More than once Bentham used the example of a doctor in this context, and urged that a physician who treats an unconscious patient ought to have a legal claim to remuneration in order to encourage similar unsolicited acts in the future. From this point of view, it is not the content of common law that is at issue in each instance, for Bentham, but whether utilitarian legislation is a habitual occupation. Legislation which cannot be traced to assignable legislators is arbitrary (V, 556).

A correspondingly practical argument against the lawyers' claim that they discover the law centers on the matter of compliance. Utility is a formal procedural principle; it ensures that all desires are taken into account when laws are made. When a law causes suffering and disrupts expectations, as every law must, it makes a difference that the injury is the outcome of utilitarian calculations. And correspondence between the language of the law and desires is one form of evidence that the law is utilitarian, Bentham thought; this correspondence reconciles men to the law. But decisions arrived at according to precedent do not speak the language of sensation, even if they conform to what utility would recommend. Common law neither refers to concrete desires as its rationale nor appeals to them for its force. If common law is coincident with utility, it should give up its "technical" tongue, for where it is not literally translatable into the language of sensation, it conceals a hidden meaning. Bentham believed, of course, that the technical language of common law consists of fictions whose meaning could not be translated into the language of sensation, and that this nonutilitarian content was either blind custom—the residue of some ancient utility, which could not now be understood—or the sinister interest of the legal profession.

Bentham's attack on the brotherhood of lawyers focused on the central fiction that the law is discovered, not only to point up the difference between common law and utilitarian legislation, but also because the entire English legal profession *qua* profession was based on this fiction. Lawyers are not rewarded for making law, but for private services—for counseling clients or arguing their cases before the bench. And there is a conflict between these private services and utility. Only in a system where judges discover the law out of the facts and legal arguments presented by counsel is counsel necessary. The need for lawyers could certainly be reduced with a utilitarian code of law, Bentham thought. The law would as nearly as possible be "there," and only the facts would require presentation; the judge himself might collect evidence. Similarly, the profession would be restricted if the judge made law outright and pronounced it on the spot; this is arbitration, or "conciliation," and Bentham contemplated a system of "domestic" justice. In either case, there would be little need for counsel to present legal arguments.

Bentham worked to explode the fiction that the law is discovered, then, because lawyers' professional services—presenting evidence and making legal arguments—rest upon this fiction. And these services, he believed, were public disservices. Where evidence is concerned, lawyers are like priests. They solicit confidences from their clients but are not compelled to reveal information to the court. They conceal evidence, discourage truth-telling, and impede justice (IX, 590). It is one thing for the court to do without information because men refuse to speak or lie; some things cannot become public knowledge without compliance. It is another thing for the state to license a profession whose services consist of aiding mendacity. The common-law system of evidence does nothing to encourage honesty and everything to encourage timidity (VI, 254). Under the guidance of priests and lawyers, Bentham wrote, men acquire the habit of perjury (V, 326). In the same vein, when lawyers argue the law of a case, they appeal to precedents that are in their client's interest. A practicing lawyer, in Bentham's phrase, is a man who "is ready to prove black white for anybody for a guinea" (X, 237). A lawyer's profession, as Bentham saw it, involves a vow of allegiance to the fraternity rather than a vow of knowledge or public service. A lawyer's tie to the brotherhood is stronger than his commitment to the rational functioning of the law. For it is only from among the arguments counsel makes as to how the facts of a case conform to some precedent that the judge discovers the law. The same rules are not, by this procedure, applied equally in every case. Lawyers and the legal ethos may conflict. In practice, common law is not general law but the mandates of a judge directed at and confined to particular individuals. In the pay of a litigant, Bentham insisted, a lawyer "acts under the impulse of an interest incurably adverse to the several ends of justice" (IX, 592).

Bentham also marshaled material arguments to show the opposition between the legal profession and legal values. He knew that the evils of litigation were not equitably borne; the present fee system on which procedure is based favors the rich. The law is an instrument of oppression, he wrote; the court is a "justice-shop," where for a sufficient sum anyone can purchase a subpoena and inflict suffering on whom he pleases (VI, 101). Moreover, the legal fraternity's professional services, already demonstrated to be public disservices, are frequently private disservices as well. The lawyer's client may be his victim. As Bentham's famous trio of evils tells it, parties at law regularly suffer vexation, expense, and delay. All professions establish the system of procedure and remuneration in their field, and the legal profession successfully maximizes fees, minimizes effort, and worst of all—and unlike the medical profession—makes business (II, 209). Bentham added new import to the notion of Parliament as a High Court when he described its collusion in the court fee system. Lawyers and judges are simply without "anxious sensibility," he wrote, and Hazlitt echoed Bentham when he said of Lord Eldon, "no act of injustice puts him beside himself."[6] Lawyers are a "gang of robbers," "licensed to be without licence," "mercenaries," and "hired killers" (V, 448, 350-351; IX, 594, 596). Clearly, Bentham's personal experiences in Chancery aroused his fiercest and most self-righteous comments, for the only reward he received for his spiritually anguished apprenticeship was insight into this powerful fellowship (V, 349). He was bitter, and voiced despair that this particular set of professional affections could be exploded (X, 77).

The majority of the people is in "a state of outlawry," Bentham charged (II, 202; V, 353n.). And outlawry is a consequence of the present character of the legal profession, quite apart from the special features of the common-law system, which heighten its injurious effects. Lawyers constitute a profession because they share a common language; Bentham called them a tribe (I, 254). Indeed, this language alone constitutes their special knowledge, not knowledge of the law. For in a noncommon-law system, the law is presumed to be known or knowable to anyone; in a common-law system, even the lawyer cannot know in advance of the judge's decision what the law will be. Briefly, a private language—the peculiar language of procedure—forms both the lawyer's knowledge and the professional bond. All professions have a common language which is incomprehensible to the uninitiated, Bentham knew. But only the legal profession's language is a ritual language, "mere words." It is like the mysterious ritual tongue of priests, he wrote. Only by speaking it to one another, by uttering magic words, can lawyers get the law to attend to men's causes. Procedure is the way to justice, and only by the incantation of these magic words is the outcome of a cause, whatever it may be, legitimated. Lawyers, like priests, are the intermediaries between men and judgment. Their rituals require that parties be regularly excluded from the judge's presence; men may not and cannot speak for themselves. Bentham made a distinct appeal for a reformation in the law, beginning with the legal profession and its procedure, its tongue.

Bentham resembled his radical French contemporaries most in the passages where he compared lawyers to priests and where his arguments were psychological. He showed that lawyers, like priests, deal in hope and fear. Priests are given credit for their belief to the extent that others feel doubt—psychologically as well as logically, doubt and belief require each other, Bentham knew. The legal profession's status rests on a similar uncertainty about the law, about what it is and how it can be brought to punish or protect men. To the extent that men cannot act for themselves, they trust others, and the legal fraternity's vow of knowledge is simultaneously a vow to maintain public ignorance. Indeed, the resemblance between lawyers and priests was not restricted to means, in Bentham's mind, but extended to the range of their power. There is no limit to the matters that come under the attention of either profession, he thought, for practically no action in the modern state is without legal consequence. It is impossible for laymen to know what the law is or how to bring justice to bear; nor can they know how to guard against future litigation. In economic affairs, above all, Bentham would agree, men must consult a legal "father confessor" at every contingency.[7] Altogether, the profession had achieved the "perfection of oppression" (II, 395).

Reformation was absolutely necessary, Bentham thought. In a common-law system lawyers manipulate evidence and precedent. Both facts and law must conform to the formulae and arguments presented by counsel, and neither client nor judge uses his own words; they speak through lawyers in their special tongue. And in every legal system, lawyers control procedure—access to justice. In this context, the result is frequently a failure of justice. But that is not all. Another effect was to encourage dishonesty, or at least make sincerity impossible. Nothing mattered more to Bentham; honesty is the chief element of responsibility and the only personal quality he focused upon. The profession did not serve the cause of legal responsibility. Indeed, when the legal profession threatened honesty, it threatened the whole idea of utilitarian legislation as well. Legislation is a matter of expressing and satisfying desires; it is only possible if both people and officials are in the habit of speaking for themselves, in words that aim at common understanding.

Bentham's assaults were not yet exhausted, however; lawyers were not the only brotherhood whose activities were in opposition to responsible public service. Indeed, he frequently juxtaposed his attack on the legal profession to his less virulent, but in some respects more profound, criticism of aristocratic officialdom. The charges he leveled against the two were complementary: lawyers usurped and abused legislative power; aristocratic officials abdicated it. "Everybody's business," he lamented, "is nobody's business" (III, 506). Much is gained by considering the two side by side (I, 244). Like professionals, aristocratic officials constitute a fraternity. But the basis of their brotherhood is not what it is for professionals, common language. And lawyers have another advantage over the nobility: if their *esprit de corps* is antisocial, still, by their professional activities, they acknowledge a regular relation between service and reward. By contrast, the present basis of aristocratic officialdom as Bentham saw it is merely shared political place, though he knew that officials were not content with this ignoble characterization of their bond. They claimed honor as their distinguishing mark, not officeholding simply. Bentham attacked aristocratic officialdom from two standpoints, then. One was aristocratic officials' lack of professionalism. The other was their pretense of honor. Theirs was neither the classical honor that attached to virtue nor the traditional aristocratic honor that attached to birth. Theirs was a degenerate notion of honor, entirely inadequate to bind and regulate officialdom.

Aristocratic Officialdom

For most reformers, the attack on aristocratic government was necessary because things had gotten worse, and their stated objective was to restore a lost constitutional balance or purity.[8] Bentham too became convinced that corruption had increased; he even spoke fearfully of "national ruin" (I, 245; III, 438).[9] Nevertheless, it was not political deterioration

127

simply that inspired his attack. His tone not so much outraged or despairing as it was ironical. For his attack was possible and made sense because what had chiefly changed, in his view, were the ideas of aristocratic officials themselves. During his lifetime, he had witnessed the defenders of aristocratic officialdom open the subject of officeholding and its reward for public discussion. Burke, he wrote in this context, had exposed his flanks and laid his principles open (V, 282). Officials had joined in a "war of words" (V, 282), and Bentham drew his arguments against them from their own speeches. The political diatribes collected under the title *Official Aptitude Maximized* contain his responses to parliamentary speeches by Burke, Rose, Peel, and Eldon (V, 263-382). Briefly, these defenders of aristocratic officialdom insisted upon some connection between office and honor, but their speeches revealed the vacuity of their notion of honor. The result was that they undermined the chief basis for aristocratic officialdom and practically invited a new account of public service.

As Bentham saw it, any discussion of honor is evidence that the idea has lost its significance. Where honor is meaningful, there is nothing much to talk about, for there is an automatic coincidence between honor and its observance; there is a coincidence between its internal form—dignity or pride—and the external mark of its recognition—esteem. Honor understood as rank or noble birth is simply 'there.'' So is the honor of virtuous character. The rules that governed grants of title as a reward for acts of courage, for example, were fixed; in Bentham's words, striking exploits "carry their own proof with them" (II, 230). To be sure, he agreed that honors should be proclaimed in order that they might be observed, but something is amiss when honor is actually solicited from the public as one's due. Further, when honor refers, as it traditionally had, to what a man is—his rank or personal qualities—any lack of external recognition is supposed to be tolerable, for honor is characteristically regarded as its own reward. Pride, Bentham insisted, does not deign to explain itself; delicacy prevents men from demanding esteem. Thus, the speeches by Burke, Rose, Peel, and Eldon soliciting public esteem for aristocratic officials signaled the dissolution of the idea of honor, and Bentham had only to point out the consequences. Honor no longer referred to pride in character or birth; instead, it pointed to some purely external reward. And all of the speakers talked as if honor were a reward that could be claimed from the public for services rendered. In this view, office was no longer its own reward, as it had been when public service was believed to affect the performer's character or earn him salvation. Now, even aristocratic officials looked at public service in terms of its effect on the recipient, and claimed honor as payment in return. With this, officialdom had entered, no matter how hesitantly or with what intent, onto the grounds of utility, where honor proper has no place.

Bentham had no doubt that this tentative venture onto utility's turf was hypocritical. Burke was the most principled of the four speakers, in his view, but Burke's principles did not include utility. With "matchless artifice," Burke merely flirted with allusions to services and the public that receives them for his own purposes, weighing his words carefully to allow for a retreat (V, 299). But at least Burke had the welfare of the state in view. By contrast, Peel and Eldon were simply unprincipled. Their professions that officeholding was a service and honor the public's reward to its servants were just that—professions, or vows—and Bentham gave them as little credence as he gave all oaths. They served only to show the distance between a true professional understanding of service and a profession that is "mere words" (IX, 60-61). Peel and Eldon were defenders of aristocratic officialdom self-consciously on the defense, Bentham thought, and they sensed the danger of the utilitarian ground that they dared not abandon (V, 377). He would have appreciated and applied to them Hazlitt's estimate of the "reformer" Brougham, who "grew scared of the sound himself had made."[10] Rose stood out in Bentham's mind as a sincere defender of rank and honor, but Rose was self-deluded: he seemed unaware that the language of utility, which crept into his speech alongside the traditional assurances of officials' dignity and appeals to popular generosity, only hastened the dissolution of honor.

Bentham's line of attack against aristocratic officialdom was presented to him, in short, by these speeches. They were, he claimed, hypocritical In fact, it is not honor that the speakers want from the public as reward, but money. Nor can the money they receive be described as reward for services, because aristocratic officials do not for the most part perform services. Their offices are sinecures at best; the benefits they reap are the result of predatory exaction.

Official Aptitude Maximized considers with some care the fate of honor. One quite obvious change Burke and the others made in the notion of honor was that they turned to the public as its source. The people are called upon not only to observe honor, which was always thought to come from God, the crown, or one's peers, but also to bestow it (IX, 78).[11] Bentham objected that this appeal to the people was purely rhetorical. For example, Burke, the "principled" defender of aristocratic officialdom, was embroiled in a battle with the crown, the traditional source of honor.[12] Bentham was certain that Burke's appeal to the people was merely a gesture, part of his effort to make officialdom and parliament men in particular independent of any undue influence by the crown. He had no doubt that Burke intended officials to be equally independent of the people. The best way to prove that Burke was hypocritical in speaking of honor as a reward for services was to look at what public service is, Bentham thought. In his view, most public services do not consist of striking exploits like acts of courage; the acts that contribute most to the welfare of society are a train of daily actions, a uniform and steady course of conduct (II, 230-231). How is the public supposed to reward these services when ordinary matters of public business are not publicized, and when Burke had no intention of allowing official behavior to be scrutinized? Bentham recognized that many public services are simply not amenable to reward in the form of public honors, for no single fact, or act, or circumstance can stand as proof of virtue when services fall within the line of ordinary actions.

He pointed to another change which had taken place in the idea of honor. In the past, it was character that was deduced from a man's rank, but these speeches defended both noble officeholders and officials from "respectable" families (V, 306-307). Almost imperceptibly, the public has been called upon to honor the occupants of office—whoever they might be and whatever their personal qualities—on the assumption that as officials they perform public services. Honor is claimed axiomatically on behalf of officeholders per se (II, 230, 412), Bentham observed, and he used Peel's speech to demonstrate this. Peel speaks of the honor of police magistrates, but the measure of honor Peel applies is not utility, for nowhere does he make reference to determinate services. Yet, in Peel's speech, honor has nothing to do with rank or character either, though in the past these have always been its accompaniment. The speech shows that it is not the public that bestows honor on officials at all, Bentham argued. Honor attaches automatically to office, and is pronounced by officials about themselves (II, 424). In this respect, officials imitate the classical brotherhood of honorable men, which was based on the mutual recognition of peers, only here mutual regard is axiomatic. In the chronicles, one portrait served for many worthies, Bentham recalled; likewise, for all official men high and low, there is one general character for excellence, tinged here and there with a little difference of color corresponding to the nature of the department (V, 330). Honor acts as

neither an incentive nor a reward; it has been reduced to eulogistic formulae. The only personal quality it points to is vanity. (Bentham observed
too that this sort of factitious honor, the bond of so many brotherhoods,
is seldom content with distinction. It typically exhibits hostility toward
outsiders as well; he referred more than once to honor among thieves, I,
428.)

In Bentham's account, aristocratic officials are stranded between two
worlds. They do not really look at services in terms of their effects on the
public happiness—for which they might conceivably claim reward. But
neither do they look upon service as its own reward, that is, as a way to
exercise virtue or earn salvation. This is an important development and
forms the crux of Bentham's attack. Aristocratic officials continue to assert their purity: "The world of politics," Bentham mocked, "is, by the
acknowledgement of both parties, divided into two opposite regions; the
world of major, and the world of minor purity" (X, 81; IX, 60). Indeed,
officials go so far as to claim that officeholding is a sacrifice: office keeps
men from their private affairs, Burke asserted. But they are not satisfied with pride in this sacrifice, and they do not consider it their distin-
quishing mark. For in fact, all four defenders of aristocratic officialdom were seeking increased monetary remuneration for officials, and
talk of honor and sacrifice was meant to add force to demands for
money. The language of honor was used quite simply to raise the price of
services. Honor, officials' counterfeit coin, was a medium for purchasing
other goods—among them the financial security that accompanies a
place. "If he [the official] sees that the *state* takes no detriment, the *state*
must see that *his* affairs should take as little," Burke wrote (V, 293).

Bentham found Burke's confession striking. He did not tire of pointing out that it marked the emptiness of the notion of honor and with it
the dissolution of the chief basis of aristocratic officialdom. If honor was
never truly disinterested, at least traditional claims of purity indicated
that honorable men tried to put a distance between themselves and the
ordinary desire for money. Honor was supposed to be a substitute, and a
higher one, for other satisfactions. In France, even the lower classes have
a feeling for honor and know its characteristic sign—contempt for
money. English law reflects this changed attitude and counts honor for
nothing, Bentham wrote: it sees no other evil in the loss of reputation
than the loss of money that is its consequence (I, 542). He directed a
devastating query at these defenders of aristocratic officialdom: is nobility less noble, respectability less respectable, in proportion to wealth? (V,
307) Aristocratic officialdom does look to the public—not to bestow or

observe honor, though, but to give up money. Wealth is the benefit sought from office. Only Rose thought of money as a way to keep up the appearance of nobility (V, 268); he subscribed to the view that a peerage without a fortune is a burden (II, 201). His inclinations were genuinely aesthetic; stationed for so long a time on the other side of the door, Bentham wrote, observing with longing the ribbons and titles of the Duke of Portland, the Earl of Liverpool, the Lord Viscount Castlereagh, Rose admired and sought to emulate aristocratic tastes. Bentham charitably admitted that Rose was "sincere." Rose actually set the value of an office by the rank and taste of its occupant. But Peel and Eldon talked of honor only in order to raise the price of services (V, 268). Money was everything to them; office was an instrument of their greed. Taken together, the speeches proved that aristocratic officials had begun to treat themselves as economic men and had altered the terms of service and reward. This is the main argument Bentham makes in *Official Aptitude Maximized, Expense Minimized:* in the arithmetic of high situation, honor and power count for nothing.

Still, differences among the speakers were important to Bentham and he was careful not to obscure them. Rose was self-deluded; Peel and Eldon were hypocritical; but Burke was principled, and he interested Bentham most. Bentham referred to himself, somewhat ironically, as Burke's "junior and survivor' (V, 282). Burke had, after all, initiated discussions of public economy and of salary as a productive reward (II, 198), and Bentham struggled to explain Burke's thoughts on economic reform. The nature of public service and the sort of men who ought to perform it seemed to converge in Burke's mind so that established wealth actually constituted both. Men of established wealth who are willing to "sacrifice" and neglect their private business and the domestic affairs of their great families are the sort who ought to occupy office. And the service they perform is precisely that they fill office, thus protecting the state from men of "ostentatious ambition," from adventurers who might rise to power via the crown or the people. In his speech on economic reform, Burke recommended the retention of sinecures: if incitements to virtuous ambition are cut off, he warned, the savings to the public will be illusory (V, 290). Men who appear selfless and offer their services gratuitously might come to power and bleed the nation (V, 282, 291-292). The pretense of heroic virtue is the surest indication that a man belongs to the lists of "base and corrupt profligates" (V, 296), Burke claimed. Established wealth is not merely an assurance of merit, in this view, it is merit.

This, Bentham admitted by the fierce tone of his reply, is a powerful argument; it is, however, wrong. Burke's concern for property caused him to make what Bentham described as a common error; he confused "obstructive circumstances" with "promotive causes" (VIII, 277) of national prosperity. Burke imagined that the prosperity of the state lay in its very abuses and that protection of property could result from "robbing" the public. This does not mean that Bentham was opposed to officeholding by men of wealth. He entertained the idea of the sale of offices, for example.[13] Even though he was convinced that poverty and ambition were the most reliable motives for getting business done, and that men of established wealth (and established indolence) would not as a rule make the best public servants, he was reconciled to their power in practice. Men of wealth, he agreed, were a "natural aristocracy". In ordinary times, rank and wealth would most likely conciliate voters (II, 312; III, 447): "When the greatest possible freedom is given to popular suffrage the species of merit people in general are best qualified to judge and most disposed to esteem, is wealth" (II, 249). In any case, there was no inevitable opposition between wealth and merit in Bentham's mind, and the distinction between wealth and merit was not the crucial issue separating him from Burke. What divided them was the distinction Bentham made between merit and favoritism.

Burke simply misrepresented the sort of men who hold office, Bentham thought. They are not for the most part men of established wealth; instead, they are men who look upon office as a way to wealth. They do not neglect their private business; they turn officeholding into a business. In practice, Bentham asserted, fortunes are made in office (V, 290), if not always for men of great families themselves, then for their friends and relations. Officialdom is not exactly a true fraternity after all. It is not made up of equals or peers but of dependents, tied by need or gratitude to those who bestow the favors of office upon them.

Peel's speech demonstrated the system at work perfectly; vague talk of honor and merit could not conceal Peel's true objective. He introduced his police magistrates' salary-raising bill by commending the present magistrates for the satisfactory way they had executed their duties, but he proceeded to recommend changing the qualifications and raising the salary attached to the post. Peel's desire was to fill the offices with barristers, whom he distinguished from the "refuse of the bar" and from local unpaid magistrates (now unaccountably deficient in aptitude). Bentham thought he knew what lay behind Peel's move; what really distinguished barristers in Peel's view was that they disdained the present salary. Peel was seeking the most avaricious candidates for police magistrate because under the present system the value of higher office is determined by what can be pocketed in lower ones (V, 268, 339, 352). The language of honor Peel used has not cost the public nothing, then; it has raised the price of services (II, 201). "According to usage, the sum is left blank in the bill," Bentham observed, "according to usage, the blank is filled up by the eloquence of the minister" (V, 329). Parties made absolutely no difference here, he added; they had not produced an "internal public" to contest rewards (II, 310). What the "ins" have in possession, the "outs" have in expectancy (IX, 74). No question of the sacrifice of private business really arises, then. Public service is a private business. Aristocratic officials lack both the professional's notion of service and the economic man's sense of business. Officialdom operates on the basis of favoritism whose end, even for men of established wealth, is money-making. The speeches document not isolated instances of corruption, Bentham insisted, but a system of corruption (IX, 66). The province of reward, Bentham thought, is the last asylum of arbitrary power, and he did not mean to refer to the crown alone.

Burke was alert to favoritism and corruption when they involved the influence of the crown on Parliament, Bentham knew. Still, Burke supported the ties of gratitude that form a system of favoritism; indeed, he wanted to encourage these ties among the great families and their dependents, who he hoped would make up and control Parliament and officialdom generally. Burke considered it part of the constitution and reason of state that means exist to reward public service tangibly, and in addition to "the *daily wages* it receives during the pleasure of the crown" (V, 287n.) For Burke, the control of favors was a constitutional concern. Bentham wrote relatively little about the relationship between crown and Commons, however; he was no advocate of balance, which suggested to him only immobility (III, 450). The one separation of power that seemed significant to him was between legislative and judicial power, and he was less concerned to protect the courts from politics than he was to point out the distinction between responsible legislation and common law (IX, 181-189). Still, he admitted that there was "something" in the use of rewards to balance a mixed constitution (II, 202). If the English constitution no longer appeared to him to be the best possible arrangement, it was, at least up until the arrangements in America, the least bad of actual constitutions (I, 240; IX, 187). And what was good in it did stem from the House of Commons. But by Burke's system, the constitution would be equally "subverted" (III, 507). Burke wanted an "immediate depression of force in the hands of the adversary, and at the same time the eventual

preservation and increase of the same force in the hands of the assailants''
(V, 282-283). He recommended merely a shift in the fountain of reward
from the crown to the great families in Parliament. Whichever way dependence and gratitude flowed, Bentham thought, they could not
produce public services. However the separation of power is made among
officials, "corruption may unite them" (IX, 123). In neither case could
Parliament perform its constitutional duty of sitting in perpetual judgment over the conduct of functionaries (III, 491). British India was an
example of the pure rule of aristocratic Parliament: it was corrupt, and
anyone who brought abuses to light suffered ruin for it (IX, 195).
Eldon's speech exposed Parliament's collusion in the favoritism and
fraud that marked the Chancery court system (V, 348, 353). By setting
court fees, Eldon had taken over the tax power of Parliament, against the
law and for his own gain. After long delay and with obvious reluctance,
Parliament looked into the matter, and used the cover provided by common law to avoid taking action against Eldon. Parliament simply supposed that, because the practice was a long-standing one, some ground
must have appeared to former judges upon which this fee setting was
consistent with the law; authorities "must be considered as having sanc-
tioned it" (V, 355, 362, 265). This outcome was not surprising, Bentham
thought; Parliament was, after all, a High Court and an ally in Eldon's
adventure. The only thing gained by the Eldon case was a clear view of
Parliament's complicity in the system. The control which it ought to have
over the conduct of ministers was entirely lost, whether the crown controls Parliament or Parliament controls government through a system of
favors.

Above all, Bentham wanted to show that Burke's desire to make Parliament independent of the crown signaled at the same time its independence of the people. Bentham did not explain his own ideas on the proper
relation between Parliament and public here, although this relation
rather than the one between Parliament and crown marked the modern
state. His political object was to expose Burke's appeals to the people as
hypocritical. Burke feared the people. He trimmed pensions while maintaining sinecures because the pension list was likely to be published and
scrutinized; he supported the "secret hand" (V, 289-290). Bentham's
judgment was severe: Burke's was the weak system of insecure men.
Hoping to be free of the crown, its old support, but afraid of the people,
Burke's aristocratic officialdom was torn between two political worlds
just as it was between the world of honor and the world of economic
principles. Defenders of officialdom who appeal to the people, Bentham

remarked, do so out of a "mixture of magnanimity and weakness" in unknown proportions (IX, 178). Eldon sensed only the weakness of his position, and his response to the charges against him was to stir up fear and resistance in his peers; he warned: "if every man who occupies a high official situation . . . is to become the object of slander and calumny, then your lordships may lay your account with similar treatment" (V, 377).

Apart from Burke's attachment to established wealth, Bentham could not discern the "principled" Burke's principles of service and reward. Burke encouraged friendships among political men, hoping, as he put it, to keep them in the habits of right and wrong in which they began life (V, 291), but Bentham could not tell exactly what these habits were except for antimonarchicalism. The distance between himself and Burke was clear. He was concerned that the business of legislation get done. He was even willing to sacrifice the impeachment power of Parliament if maintaining it meant that Parliament would concentrate on its "inferior" judicial duty to the neglect of legislation (V, 504). Indeed, Bentham was so concerned about effective legislation that he departed from the radical stand on annual Parliaments by proposing, among other things, the continuation of motions from one sitting to another (IX, 170). Burke, by contrast, did not speak about parliamentary activity at all except as a control on the executive; he had no principle of legislation, so it was no wonder that he had no principle of reward. Bentham attacked Burke directly: the public business was better off in the hands of "aspiring and needy courtiers" than in the hands of Burke's gentlemen and their dependents. Were it not for courtiers, "children of corruption," the business of state would stagnate entirely. The crown itself, he wrote, is not a perfect sinecure (III, 506). Virtually the only official exempted from Bentham's contempt was the notorious excise man, one of the few agents of central government policy (III, 505).[14] Bentham's main point here was that Burke's system based on great families was not only morally but also institutionally weak. His chief argument against favoritism was that the system did not produce policy. By itself, favoritism confers benefits, Bentham admitted, and no matter what its shape the receipt or conferral of a benefit is evil only on account of its effects (IX, 66). The evil of aristocratic officialdom and its system of reward was, in a word, impotence (IX, 187). One historian has described English government as a mix of oligarchy and anarchy;[15] he echoed Bentham, for whom it was "a mixture composed of monarchico-aristocratical despotism, with a spice of anarchy'' (IX, 153). In this system, again, ''everybody's business is no-body's business'' (III, 506).

Underlying all of Bentham's charges of favoritism and fraud was a powerful argument against Burke, Rose, Peel, and Eldon. Aristocratic officials were really economic men talking the antiquated tongue of honor. Rose alone took honor seriously; he did not understand that in a world of economics no generosity is called for on either side (V, 304). For Burke, wealth itself was clearly meritorious, but despite his concern for property he did not subscribe to economic principles, and Bentham accused him of being insensitive to the real causes of national prosperity. Every office and fee, Bentham insisted, is a tax on the wealth of the peo-ple: ''Reward can only be derived from the labour of the people and con-tributions levied on their property'' (II, 204). For every noble family kept up by pensions and sinecures, Bentham wrote in a rare example of class analysis, another family, neither noble nor respectable, will be pressed down into the ranks of the indigent (V, 306). But as usual his main argu-ment was that everyone would suffer. The crown had used up its lands creating honors, he recalled; if notions of permanent rewards and gener-osity were adhered to, Parliament might swallow up the whole produce of national industry (V, 306; IX, 79), for Burke looked upon the people's property as ''a perpetual fund of premiums'' (V, 283). Bentham did not harbor immediate apprehension for the national prosperity; his point was that Burke's notion of reward did not contain limits of any kind and that it marked out at least the ''road to national ruin'' (III, 435). Talking honor but without pride, wanting wealth but ignoring economic princi-ples, aristocratic officialdom was caught between two worlds. Aristo-cratic officials laid themselves open, Bentham wrote, to the ''combined imputations of improbity and extravagance'' (V, 282). They united in themselves the worst of both worlds.

There was irony, Bentham observed, in the fact that aristocratic offi-cials looked to office for money in this way. The depravity of the lower orders, the desperate desire for wealth which Burke feared so, had in-fected his own order. The desire for wealth without labor is a real danger, but it is not only the poor who are liable to be seduced into criminality. Peel and Eldon proved that (II, 249; IX, 62). Officialdom regularly prac-tices ''predatory exaction'' (V, 268); it is officials who are the very ''scum'' of the population, Bentham wrote (IX, 57). If ''democracy snig-gered'' at Burke's countenance (X, 267), he had only himself to blame, for public opinion was ''hatched under the wing'' of the House of Commons (IX, 187). Again, Bentham's observations were positively invited by the speeches on service and reward.

Aristocratic officials exhibited the desires of economic men without their advantages, in Bentham's view. Aristocratic officialdom is not, after all, a productive class—one whose business is beneficent because it provides not only for its own preservation but for the gratification of others as well (IX, 162). But more than anything else it was Burke's notion of independence of fortune that marked the distance between aristocratic officialdom and economic men. Economic men actually live according to an understanding which Adam Smith had recently raised to the level of a system of thought: that their wealth is part of a social system. Economics subordinates men to a system of exchange. Bentham sometimes preferred to think of social intercourse as a system of mutual services, but both ideas were meant to indicate that fortune is no more independent in practice than honor. Burke's notion of independent gentlemen denied all this; it showed that he could not overcome the aristocratic delusion of separation and independence. Burke need not have feared having the productive classes enter government, for few things could be "more manifestly *inexpedient*" to them than attacks on property (V, 297). At the very least, economic men grasp the principle of competition, which is inconsistent with favoritism (V, 294; IX, 287; II 225, 228). When economy is really at issue, public services must be looked at in something of the same light as private ones (V, 294), Bentham argued, and he warned: "An upright sovereign therefore gives nothing. He buys or he sells. His benevolence consists in economy" (II, 202).[16] Pitt had proved Burke wrong by inaugurating a just and liberal system of auctioning government contracts. Competition was not a purely economic concept in Bentham's hands, though; it was psychological as well. Nothing in a system of favoritism promotes men's best efforts or ensures services, especially those susceptible to an indefinite degree of perfection (II, 235). The main point here is that in Bentham's mind economic men understand their mutual dependence and operate under the constraints of competition. They have advantages of both insight and utility over aristocratic officials.

No one is more self-conscious about these matters than professionals, however. Despite his disdain for the legal profession, Bentham objected when Burke criticized democracy in America with the quip that the people were governed by solicitors. The professional's livelihood depends upon his reputation, and his reputation depends upon the combined scrutiny of peers and public. Dependence is clear. And, in a sense, honor does act as an incentive and a reward for professionals. As this section showed, Bentham's argument against aristocratic officials was not only that they had become economic men without economic principles, but also that they had abandoned their own principle, honor. He restored a sort of honor to officialdom by using professionalism as his model for responsible public service.

Responsible Public Service

Bentham did not delineate the specific activities that constitute public service in either *Official Aptitude Maximized* or *Rationale of Reward* in the way that he did in his *Constitutional Code.* He simply observed that the relation between service and reward will be different for each office according to its function and its most common abuse (II, 237). His chief concern in both of these works was more general. He wanted to promote the view that official aptitude could be maximized and expense minimized only where this maxim was adopted: "no benefit without burden." In one sense, this maxim simply recasts Bentham's notion that all government is evil—and expensive; it points once again to efficiency as a value. The phrase "no benefit without burden" carries another meaning as well, for it refers to public servants at the same time as it refers to government services.

The benefits of officeholding were evident, Bentham thought: power, money, and factitious honor. But the burdens were not evident, for even efficient offices were sinecures in practice. Most often officials do not labor or perform public services (V, 293). One effect of "no benefit without burden," then, was to distinguish public sinecures from the productive labor of economic men. It evoked the psychology common to Bentham and the classical economists, which says that labor is painful. Bentham differed from classical economists on the crucial question of value, for in his view, utility and not labor figured as the source and measure of value. Still, he frequently used the language of labor theory, which looked upon labor alone as productive, in order to deduce and to reinforce the conclusion that officials fail to perform services because their offices are sinecures.

The term "burden" suggests physical labor in particular, and in Bentham's hands it was employed to demystify office. He meant to unintimidate the people when, almost with relish, he characterized most offices as sinecures: "Everybody, man and boy, knows how to be idle . . . ," he wrote, "[knows] what it is to pay as well as to be paid, for doing work, and all the while seeing and leaving it undone" (V, 336). He appealed to common experience, too, when he described official business as routine. Most public employment appears in his account as a sort of drudgery; at most, ordinary officials perform clerk's work—copying and making entries under headings; the only talent required of them is a fair hand. Where something, anything, is done, office is not strictly speaking a sinecure, though, even if it demands "only what a schoolboy is capable of" and only seven months a year at that (V, 381). The aptitude officials must demonstrate consists in most cases of nothing more than assiduous attention, Bentham observed, and he called assiduous attention one of the principal moral causes of correct judgment. But from the aristocratic official's point of view, even routine efficient offices are sinecures since the business is performed by deputies or volunteer subordinates. Bentham described the labor of the brain no less than of the hand as a species of drudgery which "the man of elevated station sees the propriety and facility of turning over to the base-born crowd below" (II, 481). The cost of "honor" can actually be calculated, he explained, by looking at the amount officials collect for themselves after they have paid their deputies (II, 236-237). It is a good rule of economy to employ only those who do not think themselves superior to the work, he cautioned: "Dutch florists ought not to be employed in the cultivation of potatoes" (II, 241-242). Bentham's aim here was clearly political: he wanted to diminish popular obsequiousness toward officials. This account of the nature of official business was neither his best nor his only understanding of what government requires, however. In *The Constitutional Code,* he outlined in detail an administration whose business, if routine, requires training and experience, and whose officials are selected at least in part according to the results of competitive examinations (IX, 191, 204-206, 265, 294-295, 304-313, 316).

When Bentham wrote about the upper echelons of aristocratic officialdom—judges, ministers, and legislators—the rhetoric of class became even fiercer and was distinctly combined with charges of criminality.[17] The House of Commons is a "high school of self-licensed truantism and indiscipline," which fails to perform even an "atom of service," he wrote. High offices are not merely sinecures, they are playgrounds of the aristocracy, and Bentham drew a picture of leisure and luxury. Officials look upon Parliament as entertainment: "a seat there is not less clear of obligation than a seat in the opera house"—where the obligation is not to be a nuisance to the company. Just as at the opera, a seat is taken in the House only if there is not more amusement elsewhere, and admission is had by means of a ticket "begged or bought" (II, 394). This is not to say that Bentham was an enemy of luxury; abundance is the natural consequence of the quest for subsistence, he argued (*TL,* pp. 101, 136). Nor was he an enemy of leisure. He pointed out that leisure is necessary for discoveries in the field of law as elsewhere; private men like Price, Locke, Newton, Hume, and Smith would not have done their researches if their minds had been distracted with political occupations (II, 312). His point was that aristocratic officials do not engage in the labor of thought. Bentham wanted to close the divide that traditionally separated official labor from labor commonly understood; he also wanted to describe legislation as the labor of thought. He accused most functionaries of sitting by idly; he accused high administrative officials and legislators of spending their leisure in recreation. Public service, he repeated, must be a habitual occupation.

Occupation is made habitual, Bentham explained, by a proper system of rewards and punishments, and the study of a system of rewards was his most original and sustained effort. Reward should not be a barren gratification, he began (II, 236-237). Sometimes he recommended that officials be treated like day laborers and paid for work performed. But he was aware that this method of reward might, like the current fee system, operate to encourage officials to make business (X, 336; II, 241). Alternatively, he suggested that officials be salaried, but that the salary be guaranteed against a deposit, which they would forfeit if they did not attend and perform. Absenteeism was a special bane, for Bentham (III, 508); no excuse for nonattendance would serve, he warned functionaries, including legislators, for "the professional man, the artisan, are subject to the same losses" (II, 324). Bentham's conclusion, expressed most forcefully in *The Constitutional Code,* was that no system of reward could effectively inspire officials to perform the services attached to most posts. Only punishment can produce "absolutely necessary actions," that is, assigned and determinable duties. The threat of punishment can cause men to bring passive attention to their work, which is all that is required of most offices. The punishment of removal, coupled with an elaborate system of checks within departments, is the most efficient instrument for making officials responsible (II, 204; IX, 51). Where legislation is concerned more directly, however, official aptitude corresponds to activity. Legislation requires not only probity and intellectual aptitude, but also active talent, Bentham insisted (III, 434). The threat of removal from office can inspire officials to perform ordinary duties, but this punishment is likely to operate most effectively where duties are clearly specified and where nonperformance is manifest. Punishment can inspire attendance, for example. It is also possible that "withdrawal of confidence" can act as a constraint in other less definite cases, Bentham thought, ones where error or bad judgment and not *mala fides* are involved. But this is not a punishing age, he noted. And in any case removal occurs once the evil is already done; punishment of its authors is a "sad consolation for the mischief of war" (II, 555). Punishment can go only part of the way toward securing good government. Above all, punishment cannot animate the "hidden powers"; only reward can create energy, "that superabundance of zeal, which surmounts difficulties and goes a thousand times further than commands" (I, 338). The term "energy" was as prominent in Bentham's writings on officialdom as it was in the writings of romantics. If legislation is not exactly creative, it does require active intellectual effort. It needs to be initiated. It is in any case a world apart from the ennui that marked aristocratic officialdom in Bentham's eyes. An adequate system of rewards and punishments must be able not only to control and constrain conduct, but also to engage men.

It is important to note in this connection that Bentham did not look mainly to intellectuals for legislation. He would allow them to propose specific measures, and he encouraged governments to invite their efforts, but men of genius are rare, and occasions for them to contribute legislation are rarer still. Price's Sinking Fund was a notable exception (II, 228-229, 321). Legislation must be a regular business; it requires neither wisdom nor virtue. Bentham chose to call what is required of legislators and administrators "aptitude" in preference to the "romantic appellation, wisdom" (IX, 57). Although the special sort of thought necessary to legislation is laborious, there are men who would perform it, he was convinced. And there is a discernible relation between the sort of men who ought to legislate and the nature of their reward. Public service can engage men who, "oppressed by their insignificance," are moved to distinguish themselves (II, 249; I, 281).[18]

Burke had said that "ordinary services . . . must be secured by the motives to ordinary integrity." He meant money: money is the incitement to "virtuous ambition." Only base and corrupt profligates pretend that another reward will do; only "ostentatious ambition" offers services gratuitously (V, 295, 290, 296). This is how Bentham understood Burke, and he was prepared to agree that frugality by itself is no guarantee of merit. Republics, for example, are frugal with rewards of money but prodigal with grants of power, which they bestow on men in whom they have "momentary confidence." Political ambition is as dangerous as Burke said it was: "Woe to the grateful nation" (II, 201), Bentham wrote. But Burke was wrong to denigrate the practicability of ambitions other than the desire for money in securing public services: "My notion of him [official man] . . . is that, besides *money,* there are other things that are capable of being objects of his regard" (V, 313). It is not true that he who does not possess money possesses nothing, or that he who already possesses money can want for nothing, Bentham objected. Honor is another ambition entirely. But honor must be tamed. The honor Bentham had in mind was not the factitious honor of aristocratic officialdom, but neither was it classical honor. Classical honor had perils of its own; men who desire true honor are not content with preeminence, they want to be independent—even alone with their pride. If honor does desire recognition, Bentham explained, this is "a secret which it seeks to hide from itself." Honor's delicacy is wounded by "the formalities necessary to the public proof of its existence" (II, 230; IX, 58). Precisely these proofs are necessary for responsible public service, however. The connection between true honor and pride also explains why there was traditionally no truck between honor and money: because money is simply a matter of having more or less. Honor abhors equality; it chooses marks other than wealth, and aristocratic officialdom's yearning for money had shown this desire to be inconsistent with honor. But money is necessary as an incentive to public service; on this point Bentham agreed with Burke, albeit for different reasons. Money puts a stop to illusions of independence; money makes services regular.

Bentham's model for public service was professionalism, where honor and wisdom too are tamed. Professionalism transforms honor into reputation. The distinction turns on the fact that honor had generally been a matter of character, while professional reputation is a matter of conformity to certain established external standards attached to particular services. Honor has been tamed in the professions by the introduction of money, which regularizes services and, of equal importance, provides continual proof of the professional's dependence on public and peers. There is always the danger that where fees exist, men will make business; this was true of lawyers but not of doctors, Bentham thought. The medical profession regularly sacrifices lucrative practices by discovering cures for disease (II, 212n.). Money makes services dependable, but reputation is the principal reward of professionals; their fees are indeed "honorariums" (X, 337). In short, professionalism shows the possibility of a system of reward that exists comfortably in the twilight world between honor and business. It is a system that achieves just what Bentham sought: "a solid peace . . . between pride and cupidity" (II, 217).

The professions also close the divide between passive attention and wisdom. The knowledge required for legislation is not philosophy, Bentham taught, but formal principles and statistics. Information is received from others; like legal evidence, it is "heard" (IX, 260). But like evidence, it must be actively solicited; indeed, the forms of solicitation create information just as they do evidence in the first place. Bentham indicated quite clearly that although information on many matters susceptible of legislation (especially economic ones) is presently unavailable, once government is organized to ask for it, it will be forthcoming. More to the point here, the principle of utility makes it unnecessary for each legislator to discover for himself what information is and how it can be used for lawmaking; legislation can be taught, and its principles applied to each case. A body of experience in legislative matters was, in Bentham's mind, perfectly imaginable. His favorite way of explaining the process of legislation was to compare it to medical practice (VIII, 277; I, 304; Stark I, 379; Stark III, 253). Bentham understood what many who appeal to medicine do not: that modern medicine does not begin with an ideal of health but with a notion of disease, with pathology (I, 304). Doctors try to cure disease, and often cannot; their more immediate aim is to relieve pain (IX, 126; I, 22n.). Bentham's description of the legislator's task—to endeavor first of all to remove evil or minimize disappointment —has a clear parallel in his references to medicine. Further, doctors employ means that are, in other contexts, purely painful; every law is comparable in this regard to surgery and medicines. The particular point of comparison here is that medical practice is a matter of observation and experimentation. Only by trial and error can doctors learn which drugs work or learn to distinguish "uninfluencing" from "promotive" causes of disease (VIII, 277, 209). It is precisely experience that cannot be dispensed with in the case of legislation either (III, 490-491). And experience, Bentham advised, is most likely to be the advantage administrators have over elected lawmakers (IX, 625). Administration and legislation are "intimately connected," he explained, and he encouraged administrative officials to initiate legislation and to participate in discussions (IX, 181-188, 265, 316; III, 542, 550). Ex-deputies and veteran ministers should continue on committees, he proposed (III, 490-491; IX, 170, 175). This is not to say that experience is binding, though; lawmakers must listen, and do what each case demands. There are no inflexible rules of procedure in connection with legislation. The consequences of policy are never absolutely predictable, and laws are always remediable.

This suggests that for Bentham legislation, like professional services, was never simply a matter of technique.[19] The whole question of responsibility only arises where there is room for discretion, he knew (V, 558). There are some services, he wrote, that cannot be delimited and directed, and that men cannot be punished for not performing because we cannot know what hinders their being performed (I, 338). Legislation is the sort of task that is not susceptible to direct responsibility (II, 301n.) This indefiniteness is also true, of course, of professional services. And it is in this connection that the importance of professionalism as a model of responsible service becomes clear. The client does not know exactly what he wants from the professional; the professional cannot promise to satisfy his client by winning his case or curing his illness. Responsibility is not an economic concept and the professional relationship is not an economic one; professional and client do not make a bargain. What is purchased and sold in the professions, and in public service as well, is the professional's best effort according to established professional standards. This is not to suggest that either medicine or legislation is arbitrary, however, for Bentham meant by arbitrariness something quite definite here: being exempt from having to assign reasons (V, 556).

Responsibility consists of identifying oneself as the author of actions and of stating their rationale, ne explained. Honesty should be the "animating principle" of political assemblies (II, 303). Bentham proposed that every public office, including every administrative office, should be a unitary position (IX, 215, 76); he wanted every functionary to be designable and his place in the official hierarchy to be clear (IX, 226). He called elected representatives deputies, not because the people instruct them (IX, 161, 125), but in order to emphasize that they are appointed by the people as their agents; he meant to emphasize that officials are appointed individually, that they are individually the authors of their actions, and that they are individually answerable for them. The conduct of every official should be scrutinized, he insisted; it is not sufficient that government as a whole be acceptable to the people (IX, 155, 160). Every official must be identifiable, then, and must be prepared to pronounce the rationale behind his conduct. Something of this understanding already exists in public affairs, Bentham pointed out, for even aristocratic parliament men now think that "decency" requires each member to make a show of expressing his own opinions. And the custom of assigning reasons has been followed in some parts of the law—almost exclusively in matters pertaining to police, finance, and political economy—for these are precisely the areas in which lawmakers must create everything. In these modern fields every measure is an innovation and every law is in opposition to ancient usage; thus, "it has been necessary that authority should justify itself" (I, 162). But providing a rationale for legislation is a recent development and is restricted to these few domains of state policy. "The state of language marks the progress of ideas" (I, 102n.), Bentham wrote; the police power is a new name in contrast to the military and justice, which proceed as they traditionally had, arbitrarily. To repeat, every official is responsible to the people; he must be identifiable and he must assign reasons for his actions. It remains to show, then, what Bentham thought popular control of officials was all about.

The principal mechanism of popular control was the power of removal, Bentham argued. This power would enable and even encourage popular scrutiny of government and of individual officials in particular. It was designed to protect the people from the intrusion of officials' special and sinister interests into government. Where an official is even suspect on this count, the people should withdraw their confidence and remove him, even if he is not guilty of some determinable *mala fide.* Loss of reputation is to a political assembly what suicide is to an individual, Bentham cautioned (II, 305). The people should be able, in short, to trace the cause of their suffering (IX, 43). He meant that they should be able to trace actions to identifiable officials. He was speaking of responsibility in terms of authorship, of "who" more than "what" had caused the people injury, of men rather than measures. The people should not have to endure suffering at the hands of functionaries, Bentham insisted; functionaries must be held to the "duty of urbanity" (IX, 43), and he encouraged retaliation against officials for petty verbal injuries, ill-humor, contempt, harassment, and delay (IX, 43, 501).

This point cannot be emphasized enough. Officials are responsible to the people; they are answerable to them. But that does not mean that their duty is to give effect to popular desires simply and immediately. They are responsible to the people for utilitarian legislation, Bentham thought, for good government. He made this point over and over. Deputies appointed by the people are one protection against the evil of special interests and of arbitrariness. But not even deputies, to say nothing of administrative and judicial officials, are compelled to reflect public opinion on specific matters of policy. Bentham neither advised nor encouraged the organization of public opinion for political purposes. He did not look for the participation of people in government by this or any other informal means. And he advanced the cause of radical reform by pointing out that it did not allow the people an active part in government; their power was solely one of deputation. Bentham made this argument consistently, even in his nonrhetorical *Constitutional Code:* "It is not from any particular judgment ascertained to be on any occasion actually delivered by them, that the good here looked to is expected." An election is not a method of collecting the people's views on any particular question; it is merely a method of appointment, of choosing agents (IX, 42, 98-99). The power of the people is not an actual legislative power or command, he wrote; it is not a "directly, immediately, imperatively, impressively, and coercively acting *power*" (III, 465). The people do not actually govern; for this they are "essentially unapt" (IX, 98). The analogy to the doctor-patient relationship is especially enlightening here. The legislator is supposed to listen to people for their expressions of pleasure and pain, for their symptoms. He is not bound to attend to their self-diagnoses. Perhaps one reason that Bentham preferred to speak of the happiness of the people, rather than of their interests, was to make this distinction plain (IX, 6, 125). The good that is to be expected from the judgment of public opinion, he repeated, is not from anything expected to be said by it, but from what is expected to be thought (IX, 42, 62, 204, 501). Responsible government is most likely to be obeyed.

Responsibility was only in part a matter of establishing mechanisms by which officials are made answerable for their conduct. They are responsible to the people for utilitarian legislation, and Bentham paid as much attention to the ethos of public service, which he expected would arm and engage officials, as he did to democratic control. By their composition, political assemblies have been said to comprise an "internal public," he wrote. But the happiness of individuals is inadequately ensured by this means (II, 310). The empire of lawyers had grown up in England by default, Bentham warned, because of the "interrupted, unwieldy, heterogeneous, unconnected multitude" that typically comprised lawmakers. This crew had been unable to legislate, and the law fell into the hands of that compact, experienced body of connected individuals, the judicature (*OLG*, p. 240). The homogeneity Bentham hoped for in government was not a function of the "representative" composition of government, then. He looked instead to an ethos of responsible public service as the integrative agency. Once again, the professional ethos is the model here. The professional characteristically makes his best effort according to standards common to the fraternity, and the profession as a whole conceives of its interest as the maintenance of these standards. Responsibility consists, in this view, of stating one's reasons in the language of the profession. It is just this sort of ethos that Bentham wanted officials to make their own. Bentham encouraged public scrutiny, of course, but it was equally important that the eyes of a member's "own critical and intelligent profession" (X, 337) be focused on him. Just as the professional internalizes standards which are largely self-enforcing, Bentham looked to another sort of "internal public" to make officials responsible: officials should, he wrote, "keep up the habit of considering their conduct as exposed to scrutiny" (II, 426). Much as he loathed oaths, Bentham would have legislators take one fashioned after the Hippocratic oath (IX, 198-199). He knew, though, that the acceptance of common standards and their internalization comes first of all from having learned and used the professional language, that great fraternal bond.

As is well known, Bentham gave considerable thought to the language legislators (and all government officials) ought to use, to what would be in effect their professional tongue. He spoke of it as the language of utility, or sensation. Here, too, medicine served as Bentham's illustration and makes his meaning clear. Relief and cure are impossible until there are appropriate and characteristic names to identify the causes of diseases, he wrote; medicine requires a terminology that throws light on the nature of disorder and allows it to be spoken of. This is as little a secret to practitioners on the body politic as it is to those on the body natural, he added (V, 269n.). The language of sensation directs lawmakers' attention to what they must consider and treat: the pleasures and pains of individuals. What the language and forms inseparable from utility guarantee above all, then, is that information is collected. And the whole power of the state must be exercised for this purpose (VI, 61). "Sources of information will not be wanting," Bentham was certain, "as soon as there is a competent authority to consult them (Stark, III, 171).[20] In *The Constitutional Code,* Bentham set out in detail the method by which legislators and judicial and administrative officials solicit information in fulfillment of their "statistic," "inspective," and "elicitative" functions. Perhaps Bentham's language of sensation can best be understood, however, if it is seen as a reaction against the political language of aristocratic officialdom—rhetoric.

Official Aptitude Maximized is itself a diatribe against oratory. It was addressed to the statesmen Bentham attacked, and was intended to cause them uneasiness. In this and other instances he wrote in their language, but with a difference: Burke's rhetoric was Ciceronian, the rhetoric of orthodoxy; Bentham's was irony, the tone of subversion.[21] Rhetoric,

Bentham knew, is spoken to friends; it is the tongue appropriate to aristocracies and small democracies, and Brougham's confessed object was to maintain, simultaneously, standards of public virtue and oratorical excellence.[22] In the modern state, Bentham thought, the two are in conflict, and rhetoric is simply inconsistent with responsibility as he understood it. For the whole point of oratory is to exhort, to persuade others to concur because of who or what the speaker is. Rhetoric denotes, for Bentham, as his criticism of Burke shows, a "distrust of metaphysics" (X, 510). The end of rhetoric is not to educate men but to come to agreement, and the orator cares not at all whether listeners understand his reasons so long as they are persuaded. Rhetoric is guided by the "regula Lesbia"; it chooses sides according to what produces agreement (V, 586n.; II, 465). At present, Bentham wrote, parliament men speak many different tongues: there are orators for those easily captivated by the strength of lungs and not argument; satirical orators for those whose object is to be amused; reasoners for the few who yield only to reason (that is, "artful and enterprising men" who scour the country and calculate votes); and those adept in the current vogue of fiscal speeches—pseudo-science (V, 385-386). Oration, in short, is supplication (II, 327); it wants agreement. But if rhetoric can produce agreement, it cannot produce understanding. And the point of utility, as of any scientific language, is precisely to present reasons to the end of understanding. Utility is, after all, a *rationale* for law.

The language of sensation ought to be the common tongue of public servants, then. Its object is common understanding, but that is all it promises. Agreement about legislation is not guaranteed to follow, Bentham admitted. Rhetoric may produce unanimity, but this is merely a surface victory: "it is such unanimity as famine and imprisonment extort from an English jury" (II, 332). The discipline Bentham looked to to produce agreement was imposed by the language of sensation and the principle of utility alone. If it does nothing else, if it cannot produce positive measures, still this language recalls the idea that "every obligation ought to bear the character of a benefit" (III, 180). More than anything else, a language which makes distinct reference to the desires of individuals would make officials responsible.

There remains this to say in conclusion. Bentham modeled his notion of public service on professionalism. A reputation for the competent application of principle replaces character in this scheme as a measure of aptitude, and responsibility is further assured by a "solid peace between pride and cupidity." Bentham's account is in every way a compromise, for professionalism exists in the shadows of knowledge and character. But the alternative, as he saw it, was a fraternity of aristocratic officials whose bond was false honor and whose object was to satisfy their greed. In his mind, a professional ethos promised to be an improvement. Bentham's account is a compromise, too, because professional reputation is a mix in uncertain proportions of the opinions of public and peers. This notion of public service is precisely a balance between modeling a legislator after a doctor and at the same time calling him a representative. The final expression of this admittedly uneasy compromise is Bentham's notion of responsibility.

This means, of course, that an entirely new problem occupies political center stage; the question debated is not the proper divide between the state and society, or between the state and individuals. The reconciliation men have to effect in this view is between experts and public. Bentham cannot be said to have worked out a solution to this problem. But it can be said of him that he did not disregard it, and even that he guarded against it. Although legislation is not a matter of putting popular opinion directly into legal form, still it can never escape reference to the people's desires. At every point, Bentham objected to men and means that fail to ask political questions directly; that was, after all, utility's point of pride. Utility requires that desires be consulted not only initially, but always. Legislation has no end. That is why administrative and judicial officials as well as elected representatives are responsible. In fact, this view of legislation as a continual, indecisive, and unlimited process is just what makes utility unbearable to some.

Conclusion

The argument of this book is that Bentham's political thought forms a theory of the modern state. In most state theories, the state is conceived as a higher rationality which stands above the changing and conflicting interests of individuals or groups. Bentham called this rationality utility. And he explained that utility finds expression in a unified system of law. A single, rational legal system gives the state its unity, he thought. The state is a legal entity; its ethical basis is individualism. This is a peculiarly modern conception of political order, Bentham claimed, and it remained for him to show how politics might be brought in line with this understanding. Modernization requires two things above all. It requires a legal system with an illimitable range, corresponding to its basis in the desires of individuals. It also requires institutions to support this legal system—especially a bureaucratized public service which makes of legislation a continual process in the effort to accommodate diversity and change.

This theory of the state as a norm of order is separable from preferences for a particular regime, including mixed government. Simply, the state absorbs diversity. Perhaps this emphasis on the state as a legal entity goes some way toward explaining why it has been so difficult to ascertain Bentham's political preferences; he does not have a definite place on the spectrum liberal-radical-conservative because his main concern was to comprehend the requirements of the state, or of good government, and insofar as he preferred democracy, he did so for purely

151

instrumental reasons. The one thing he did insist on (and it followed from the state's basis in individualism, in his view) was absolutism. This is not to say that Bentham was a proponent of what is now referred to as the strong state, however. Utility is a formal principle, but it is informed by definite values which are unmistakable in Bentham's work.

Bentham is one of the great proselytizers for legalism as a value. Happiness and justice are inseparable, he argued, for both depend on rule following where there is a rational system of law. He also set out plainly the objectives attached to legalism as a value—security of expectation and personal responsibility. Legalism is not the only value that informed utility as a rationale for law, though. The other is diversity, or toleration. Bentham did not promise that utility would prevent disagreement or hostility; in fact, one of his claims for the principle was that it would make the grounds of disagreement clear. Utility would substitute resistance or civil war for conspiracy, he explained. Nor did he promise that utility would absolutely guarantee tolerance in practice. No legal form or formula, nothing in due process, he knew, can prevent the political persecution of obnoxious parties (VI, 108-109). But utility goes a long way toward preventing persecution, he thought. Utility does not look upon unanimity as the sole or even best basis for taking political decisions, and utility does not teach that unanimity is necessary for order. Indeed, its principal merit is that it opposes rhetorical formulae that mask the longing for unanimity. Where utility is the rationale for political conduct, it forces rulers at least to attend to all desires, and in one sense it mitigates even the evils of intolerance by making all measures remediable. Certainly, once rational discussion prevails, fanaticism will be exposed, even if it cannot be overcome in every instance. Altogether, utility is the best chance for agreement and order in the modern state. If this was a negative claim, it was not meant to be a modest one.

Bentham's thought was clearly negative and somewhat more modest on the subject of who should legislate. Despite his many writings on responsible public service, he never pointed to who exactly would serve. Only two things are certain: the state need not depend upon philosophers or outsiders and it cannot depend upon traditional elites for its rational functioning. Bentham could not say who the *novi homines* were except that they were active men, presumably from the middle class. He did say too that the organization of government and the ethos of public service would make officials responsible. But like tolerance, responsibility is a personal habit, and like tolerance, it is not a quality likely to be more commonly found in rulers than in anyone else. Tolerance will only be the mark of public policy where men generally are reconciled to diversity, he knew; responsibility will prevail in public service only where the people generally are suspicious.

Perhaps the optimism Bentham felt about the state as a norm of order can also be understood best in a negative light. Not everyone is always or even equally served by utility, he admitted; his stock phrases—government is an evil, and the principle of nondisappointment—make this clear. But the state can secure men better than any other form of order, he was convinced, and this attitude is manifest in his writings on international affairs. No principle can absolutely prevent disagreement or even war, but when concern for the best interest of state governs the conduct of rulers, foreign affairs are bound to be conducted more moderately than when they are inspired by religious or dynastic quarrels or by national animosities. In both international and domestic affairs, Bentham argued, modern politics turns on an estimation of the consequences of actions for the happiness of individuals in the state. The promise utility holds out is of efficiency. It looks to minimize evil. In fact, the main point of Bentham's diverse practical recommendations for reform was to make the costs as well as the advantages of taking the state as a norm a matter of common understanding. This new public rationality called utility must be public, he insisted. The exigencies of utility must not be secreted, not even to keep the peace or to spare the public conscience. The state can protect men better than any other form of order, and it is the best norm of order on another count as well: it is the idea most likely to reconcile men to diversity and change, which are the inevitable marks of modernity.

Notes

Index

Notes

Introduction

1. Ernst Cassirer, *The Myth of the State* (New Haven: Yale University Press, 1946).

2. Elie Halévy, *The Growth of Philosophic Radicalism* (Boston: Beacon Press, 1966).

3. Friedrich Meinecke, *Machiavellism: The Doctrine of Raison D'État and its Place in Modern History* (London: Routledge and Kegan Paul, 1957).

4. See David Lyons, *In the Interest of the Governed: A Study in Bentham's Political Philosophy of Utility and Law* (Oxford: Oxford University Press, Clarendon Press, 1973). Lyons gives a philosophically acute account of the principle of utility. Utility, he argues, is a dual standard whose recommendations in matters of public and private morality are different, though not necessarily in conflict. The dual standard derives from the fundamental principle that directs men to act "in the interest of the governed."

1. A Utilitarian Code of Law

1. Gilbert Highet, *The Classical Tradition* (Oxford: Oxford University Press, 1949), p. 267 and n. 7.

2. Judith Shklar discusses this standard in *Men and Citizens: A Study of Rousseau's Social Theory* (Cambridge: Cambridge University Press, 1969), pp. 224-225.

3. The expression "divided nature" is used by Shirley Letwin, *The Pursuit of Certainty* (Cambridge: Cambridge University Press, 1965), p. 183. For her, Bentham's tension was dispositional; he shifted between a condition of active benevolence, inspired by a "morbid" sensitivity to the impermanence of human things, and the stance of hermit and dreamer, whose ambition was to effect a grand and permanent synthesis of law for the world as a whole. In contrast to Letwin, Mary P. Mack discusses the stylistic differences between Bentham's arcane work on language and logic and his popular writings, in *Jeremy Bentham:*

An Odyssey of Ideas, 1748-1792 (New York: Columbia University Press, 1963). For Elie Halévy, the dualism was one of political preference; he marks Bentham's career by a shift from admiration for benevolent despotism to some sort of democratic advocacy, in *The Growth of Philosophic Radicalism* (Boston: Beacon Press, 1966), pp. 490-491. Halévy also held the influential view that Bentham's resolution of the problem of the identification of interests differed for economic and juridical matters, p. 127.

4. Cited in Graham Wallace, "Jeremy Bentham," *Political Science Quarterly,* 38 (March 1923), 47.

5. David Lyons, *In the Interest of the Governed: A Study in Bentham's Political Philosophy of Utility and Law* (Oxford: Oxford University Press, Clarendon Press, 1973), p. 4. Werner Stark, for example, modestly provides only the materials for a reevaluation of Bentham's place in the history of economic thought, in Stark, I, 11.

6. Lyons describes this pendulum of opinion, *In the Interest of the Governed,* pp. 1-3.

7. F. S. Fénélon, *The Adventures of Telemachus* (Dublin: Wilson, Slanders, Sleate, 1769), p. 202.

8. Hegel's view, by contrast, is that the ancient lawgivers were "practical politicians," in *The Philosophy of History* (New York: Dover Publications, 1956), p. 251.

9. Cited in Mack, *Bentham,* p. 8.

10. More precisely, the judge is a mixed case for Bentham. Even where the law is given to him in the form of a code, he must interpret it, or, as Bentham admits, legislate. When he does, his character is closer to that of the utilitarian legislator. See Chapter 4.

11. As Halévy maintains, this does not mean that the theory of legislation is easily understood, only that it is generally intelligible, *Philosophic Radicalism,* pp. 77-78. Bentham never disputed the labor attached to thought (I, iv; X, 470) or the division of labor; thus, there exists a place for Legislator and legislators in his account of lawmaking.

12. Plato, "Laws," in *The Collected Dialogues,* ed. Edith Hamilton and Huntington Cairns (Princeton: Princeton University Press, 1961), l. 749, p. 1325.

13. Ibid., l. 772, p. 1349.

14. Ibid., l. 664, p. 1260.

15. Where the concern is Bentham's own political preferences for one or another form of government, his readers have taken another view. See Halévy, *Philosophic Radicalism,* pp. 490-491, or Mack, *Bentham,* pp. 116, 209.

16. The phrase is reminiscent of Locke's psychology of learning, and reinforces the quotation by Bentham at the start of the chapter.

17. Letwin, *Pursuit of Certainty,* pp. 176-177, gives a full account of this.

18. Fénélon, *Telemachus,* p. 217.

19. In this vein, Bentham said of Robert Owen that he "begins in vapour and ends in smoke" (X, 570).

20. Max Weber, *Weber on Law in Economy and Society,* ed. Max Rheinstein (Cambridge, Mass.: Harvard University Press, 1954), p. 286.

2. A Social Psychology for Legislators

1. The state, then, is a legal entity which comprises this unified system of law and the institutions necessary to support it. These institutions, including representation and especially administration, are discussed in Chapters 4 and 6.

2. Ernst Cassirer, *The Philosophy of the Enlightenment* (Boston: Beacon Press, 1951), pp. 93-94.

3. John Locke, *An Essay concerning Human Understanding* (Toronto: Collier-Macmillan, 1965), p. 99.

4. John Locke, *Some Thoughts concerning Education* (New York: Barron's Educational Series, 1964), p. 175.

5. Locke, *Essay,* pp. 144, 156.

6. Cassirer, *Enlightenment,* p. 100.

7. Locke, *Essay,* p. 101.

8. Ibid., p. 169.

9. Ibid., p. 161.

10. Cassirer, *Enlightenment,* p. 101.

11. C. A. Helvetius, *A Treatise on Man* (New York: Burt Franklin, 1969), I, 114.

12. Ibid., I, 124.

13. David Hartley, *Observations on Man* (London: T. Johnson, 1791), pp. 4-37.

14. Ibid., p. 296.

15. Elie Halévy, *The Growth of Philosophic Radicalism* (Boston: Beacon Press, 1966), p. 17.

16. David Baumgardt explains the consequences for moral philosophy of Bentham's broad and neutral view of motives and of his attack on moral "rigorism" in *Bentham and the Ethics of Today* (New York: Octagon Books, 1966), pp. 253-275, 375-378.

17. A discussion of honor appears in Chapter 6.

18. It should be noted, too, that Bentham's psychology is distinguished by the force he attributes to antipathy.

19. It does, though, constrain legislators to attend especially to interests and sanctions that are measurable and comparable in the way that economic ones are presumed to be (I, 90-91). Halévy makes a similar point in *Philosophic Radicalism,* p. 15.

20. The criteria for estimating the force of sanctions have been the subject of much study, beginning with Halévy's summary in *Philosophic Radicalism,* p. 68.

21. One consequence for political thought of at least some historical psychologies had been the elimination of responsibility; this is the case, for instance, with Robert Owen's work.

22. Baumgardt cites this manuscript, *Bentham and the Ethics of Today,* p. 252.

23. These matters are discussed in W. Cook, "Act, Intention, and Motive in the Criminal Law," *Yale Law Journal,* 26 (1916-17), 646-663.

24. Cassirer, *Enlightenment,* p. 26.

25. Halévy, *Philosophic Radicalism,* p. 193.

26. Bentham did not mean to make responsibility impossible. His objection was to the practicability for politics of radical changes in men's desires.

27. Thomas Hobbes, *Leviathan* (Baltimore: Penguin Books, 1961), p. 119.

28. Ibid., p. 83.

29. Among other things, the universality of motives which psychology re veals argues against aristocratic culture.

30. Hobbes, *Leviathan,* p. 88.

31. Ibid., pp. 150, 184.

32. Bentham allowed that there is an evil of nonpossession but denied that it was a felt privation. Or if it is felt, it is restricted to individuals, and is quite different from the fear of loss, which is spread, and made general, and which he calls alarm (I, 309).

33. But given Bentham's own scheme for pauper relief, it is difficult to see any part remaining for voluntary charity. His project for a compulsory workhouse would eliminate entirely the "extortionist" activities of beggars, unlicensed hawkers, and so forth (VIII, 401). On the other hand, because the state ensures only subsistence, charity could address itself to poverty taken more broadly.

34. Bentham's objection to leaving the care of the indigent to charity turns not only on the random character of the benefits distributed, but also on the inequitable character of contributions. Charity, he observed, falls most heavily on the humane (VIII, 411).

35. The same economic contingencies that create poverty in the first place could disrupt its relief, Bentham knew. His plan for pauper relief aimed at selfsupply for the workhouses as protection against the instability of the market. See Charles Bahmueller, Jr., "The End of Contingency: Bentham on Poverty," Ph.D. diss., Harvard University, 1975.

36. Gertrude Himmelfarb argues, though, that Bentham's scheme for pauper relief treats the indigent as criminals, in "Bentham's Utopia: The National Charity Company," *Journal of British Studies,* 10 (November 1970), 80-125. The poor are forced to labor for relief, but Bentham denied this was punishment because its object was neither to deter others from idleness nor vengeance. The editor of Bentham's economic writings, by contrast, describes the measures as progressive (Stark, I, 13).

37. It is the "business of government" to promote the happiness of society by rewarding and punishing (I, 35).

38. Most often, the argument for or against state action proceeds strictly in terms of the happiness of individuals; occasionally, though, Bentham used the rhetoric of political economy proper, and equality was expressed as a problem of national production and strength. His scheme for pauper relief, for example, contains references to the national economy and defense (VIII, 368, 382).

39. Halévy, *Philosophic Radicalism,* pp. 116-117; Stark, I, Introduction, pp. 52-55; Stark, III, Introduction, pp. 32-33, 39-43; and most recently, James Steintrager, *Bentham* (Ithaca: Cornell University Press, 1977), pp. 62-76.

40. Bentham observed: not only individuals but even classes "die or sleep,"

and the continuance of many classes of entities depends upon the human will; they suffer "a precarious existence" (*OLG*, pp. 75 and 172n.).

3. Antilegal Ideologies

1. Bentham addressed this matter in "metaphysical" terms where he discussed the language of jurisprudence. This is the subject of C. K. Ogden's *Bentham's Theory of Fictions* (Paterson, N.J.: Littlefield, Adams, 1959).

2. Natural rights is the example used here because although the objects of Bentham's attack on fictions changed, he was consistently opposed to natural rights. See *Correspondence,* I, 341-343, for a very early instance of this.

3. David Baumgardt, *Bentham and the Ethics of Today* (New York: Octagon Books, 1966), pp. 404-406, 310-311.

4. J. H. Burns argues that real changes in Bentham's political preferences can be traced—from his first apolitical arguments against the fallacies of legal conservatism, to his attacks on the fallacies of revolutionary democracy (which continued until the Napoleanic Wars), followed by his attacks on political conservatism. However, there are examples of all of these throughout Bentham's writings, Burns demonstrates, and "the fact of personal identity and continuity remains." Bentham's several arguments against higher law were not strictly logical, Burns adds: Bentham attacked the political enthusiasm and language that prevented rational argument altogether. J. H. Burns, "Bentham's Critique of Political Fallacies," in B. Parekh, ed., *Jeremy Bentham: Ten Critical Essays* (London: Frank Cass, 1974), p. 155.

5. J. H. Burns, "Bentham and the French Revolution," *Royal Historical Society Transactions*, 16 (1966), 95.

6. Whether Bentham held democratic values before the revolution, or not until his attachment to James Mill in 1809, as Halévy argues, there is general agreement that the revolution moved him to consider democratic representation, at least as a speculative matter. See especially Burns, "Bentham and the French Revolution," pp. 95-114.

7. Bentham made special reference to intolerance of diverse sexual preferences (IX, 53).

8. Blackstone, Bentham argued, recognized that the notion of an original contract could be used to encourage either obedience or revolt; his formula could be either entirely conservative or revolutionary. Of course, this example does not match nineteenth-century intellectuals who alternated between revolution and reaction.

9. This looks ahead to Chapter 5 and Bentham's quite traditional thoughts on national security.

10. See Chapter 6 for Bentham's discussion of Peel's Police Magistrate's Salary-Raising Bill.

11. Ogden, *Bentham's Theory of Fictions*, p. 15.

12. It is not necessary to take Charles Tarleton's position and claim that these observations were a strategy addressed to rulers and designed to get them to care for the general interest. Charles Tarleton, "The Overlooked Strategy of

Bentham's *Fragment on Government," Political Studies*, 20 (December 1972), 397-406. It is questionable, in fact, whether Bentham always thought that rulers needed to be shown the insecurity of their position; events had made them insecure enough, and their own behavior and political formulae showed this.

13. See note 4. There remains no comprehensive biography of Bentham. The most recent work to survey these discussions of political preference and to add evidence from the Bentham manuscripts is James Steintrager, *Bentham* (Ithaca: Cornell University Press, 1977).

4. Sovereignty and Law

1. Jean Bodin, *The Six Books of a Commonweale* (Cambridge, Mass.: Harvard University Press, 1962), p. 95.

2. J. N. Figgis, *The Divine Right of Kings* (Gloucester: Peter Smith, 1970), pp. 14, 165, 238, 246.

3. Bodin, *Commonweale*, p. 84; Alexander D'Entrèves, *The Notion of the State* (Oxford: Oxford University Press, Clarendon Press, 1967), p. 101.

4. Bodin, *Commonweale,* p. 84.

5. F. M. Watkins, *The State as a Concept of Political Science* (New York: Harper & Brothers, 1934), p. 50.

6. Judith Shklar, *Men and Citizens: A Study of Rousseau's Social Theory* (Cambridge: Cambridge University Press, 1969), pp. 181, 190.

7. C. J. Friedrich, *Limited Government: A Comparison* (Englewood Cliffs, N.J.: Prentice-Hall, 1977), p. 19.

8. Elie Halévy's claim that Bentham's constitutional state has no sovereign uses the term "sovereign" in this sense to refer to monarchy, in *The Growth of Philosophic Radicalism* (Boston: Beacon Press, 1951), p. 409.

9. See H. L. A. Hart, "Bentham on Sovereignty," in Bhikhu Parekh, ed., *Jeremy Bentham: Ten Critical Essays* (London: Frank Cass, 1974), pp. 148-149, 151.

10. J. H. Burns emphasizes that Bentham's essay on representation was not a general theory of representation. And he points out that the course of the revolution caused Bentham to stop considering constitutional questions until 1809, when he wrote his *Plan of Parliamentary Reform* (it was not published until 1817). See Burns, "Bentham and the French Revolution," *Royal Historical Society Transactions*, 16 (1966), 95-114.

11. Halévy in *Philosophic Radicalism*, pp. 154, 249-251, argues that Bentham's democratical sentiments were inspired by his association with James Mill, about 1809, and this view is supported by the Introduction Bentham added to the *Plan of Parliamentary Reform in the Form of a Catechism* (III, 435-438). Mary Mack, by contrast, insists that Bentham was a full-fledged radical democrat by 1790, in *Jeremy Bentham: An Odyssey of Ideas, 1748-1792* (New York: Columbia University Press, 1963), pp. 116-117. See too Burns, "Bentham and the French Revolution," and James Steintrager, *Bentham* (Ithaca: Cornell University Press, 1977), especially chap. 4.

12. Thus, when Bentham insisted on constant attendance by deputies, his concern was not only with the representative character of the assembly, indeed it

was not chiefly that (IX, 42). Instead, he was concerned that without the presence of independent deputies the control of the House over ministers would be lost (III, 509).

13. Bentham was aware, too, that popular elections bind the people to their governors as well as the reverse. One consequence of direct elections, he wrote, is to attach the people to their deputies by connections of affection and power (II, 301). Similarly, on the matter of attendance at the assembly, it was Bentham's view that if the legislature's identity changes because of absence, you cannot speak of the "will" of the assembly, and the public may be less willing to conform to its rules (II, 324).

14. Halévy, *Philosophic Radicalism*, pp. 153-154; Burns, "Bentham and the French Revolution," observes that on the subjects of judicial responsibility and parliamentary procedure Bentham's proposals were original.

15. Sovereignty does not, as in American political thought, find expression in constitutional conventions.

16. Bentham's command theory poses special difficulties because it allows for permissive laws as well as commands. Bentham's "deontic logic" is the subject of David Lyons's *In the Interest of the Governed: A Study in Bentham's Political Philosophy of Utility and Law* (Oxford: Oxford University Press, Clarendon Press, 1973).

17. Max Weber, *Weber on Law in Economy and Society*, ed. Max Rheinstein (Cambridge, Mass.: Harvard University Press, 1954), pp. 279-280.

18. Weber, *On Law*, p. 320.

19. Lyons, *In the Interest of the Governed*, p. 120.

20. R. H. Graveson cites this quotation in "The Restless Spirit of English Law," in G. Keeton and G. Schwarzenberger, eds., *Jeremy Bentham and the Law* (London: Stevens & Sons, 1948), p. 108.

21. Weber, *On Law*, p. 59.

5. The Sovereign State

1. Bentham discusses the proper sphere of "independent sovereignty" in Essay II of *Principles of International Law*, "Of Subjects, or of the Personal Extent of the Dominion of the Laws" (II, 540-544).

2. See David Lyons, *In the Interest of the Governed: A Study in Bentham's Political Philosophy of Utility and Law* (Oxford: Oxford University Press, Clarendon Press, 1973).

3. He had in mind especially the effect of war on national wealth (Stark, III, 116-118).

4. Elie Halévy argues this in *The Growth of Philosophic Radicalism* (Boston: Beacon Press, 1966), p. 119. Carlton Hayes makes a case for Bentham as a nationalist and advocate of self-determination; but his citations do not bear him out, in *The Historical Evolution of Modern Nationalism* (New York: Richard Smith, 1931).

5. Stanley Hoffmann, *The State of War* (New York: F. Praeger, 1965), p. 60.

6. Lying always had a peculiar place in Bentham's catalogue of offenses,

and he did not absolutely proscribe it.

7. Of course, wars of conquest were also inexpedient where government was organized in such a way that only a few would profit from plunder, and Bentham seemed by this to set representative democracies apart (II, 557). However, *The Constitutional Code* continued to warn against war-mongering and profiteering, even by a democratic regime.

8. F. Meinecke, *Machiavellism* (London: Routledge and Kegan Paul, 1957), p. 172.

9. Hayes portrays Bentham as a British patriot, and on this matter his references are convincing—they range from Bentham's eulogizing of "English liberties" to his thoughts on the English language (VIII, 185-187). Bentham's self-characterization as a citizen of the world, Hayes explains, was meant to show only that he bore no antipathy toward foreigners—he was not a cosmopolitan. Hayes, *Evolution of Modern Nationalism,* pp. 127-128.

6. Responsible Public Service

1. Government ought to be organized logically to make the flow of information almost inevitable. For one example, see Bentham's account of local government and in particular the activities of the local registrar in his *Constitutional Code* (IX, 625-636). He was especially concerned with accountability within departments and with the interaction between central and local government.

2. Henry Brougham, *Historical Sketches of Statesmen Who Flourished in the Time of George III* (London: Griffin, 1855-6), I, vii.

3. *Official Aptitude Maximized, Expense Minimized* was published in 1832. The essay "Defense of Economy against Burke" was printed in the *Pamphleteer* in 1817, as was the "Defense against George Rose." They were both written in 1810. The tracts on Peel and Lord Eldon were printed in 1825.

4. This is not to say that historians agree on Bentham's actual influence on reforms, especially administrative reforms, in the nineteenth century. There is a considerable literature on both sides of the question of the importance of Benthamism for political development. See M. Blaug, "The Myth of the Old Poor Law and the Making of the New," *Journal of Economic History,* 23 (1963), 151-184; J. Hart, "Nineteenth Century Social Reform: A Tory Interpretation," *Past and Present,* no. 31 (1965), 39-61; L. J. Hume, "Jeremy Bentham and the Nineteenth Century Revolution in Government," *Historical Journal,* 10, no. 3 (1967), 361-375; O. MacDonough, "The Nineteenth Century Revolution in Government," *Historical Journal,* 1, no. 1 (1958), 52-67; H. Parris, "The Nineteenth Century Revolution in Government: A Reappraisal Reappraised," *Historical Journal,* 3, no. 1 (1960), 17-37; D. Roberts, "Jeremy Bentham and the Victorian Administrative State," *Victorian Studies,* 11, no. 3 (March 1959), 193-210.

5. He also wrote, "public virtue in this shape cannot reasonably be regarded as being so frequently exemplified as insanity" (IX, 61).

6. William Hazlitt, *The Spirit of the Age* (London: Oxford University Press, 1911), p. 210.

7. Max Weber, *Weber on Law in Economy and Society,* ed. Max Rheinstein (Cambridge, Mass.: Harvard University Press, 1954), p. 317.

8. J. R. Pole, *Political Representation in England and the Origins of the American Republic* (Berkeley: University of California Press, 1966), p. 435.

9. He always laid the blame equally with the crown and the corrupted; the texture of the system and not isolated acts of abuse was at issue for Bentham (IX, 65-66; II, 466).

10. Hazlitt, *The Spirit of the Age,* p. 204.

11. See Harvey C. Mansfield, Jr., *Statesmanship and Party Government* (Chicago: University of Chicago Press, 1965), chap. 6.

12. C. S. Montesquieu, *The Spirit of the Laws* (New York: Hafner, 1949), p. 25.

13. He would auction offices—having first ascertained that the competitors were of equal aptitude—for the same reasons that Burke would keep sinecures—reasons of economy (III, 486; IX, 287). That men would pay to serve also seemed to Bentham proof that honor does have a part in inspiring public service.

14. Bentham attacked justices of the peace in particular (IX, 524).

15. Elie Halévy, *England in 1815* (New York: Barnes and Noble, 1961), p. 588.

16. As Mary Mack indicates, Bentham did not confuse low-priced government, or economy, with cheap government; his concern was good, or efficient, government. *Jeremy Bentham: An Odyssey of Ideas, 1748-1792* (New York: Columbia University Press, 1963), p. 54.

17. Even so, Bentham did not propose their removal simply. He would assure "complete indemnity to those whose emoluments are diminished or whose offices are suppressed" by reforms. Anything else, he wrote, is pure malevolence (II, 251-252).

18. One important resemblance to classical honor remains, then, for the class is an open one and its occupants are, in a sense, self-selecting.

19. Shirley Letwin judged differently in *The Pursuit of Certainty* (Cambridge: Cambridge University Press, 1965), p. 187.

20. Bentham's preoccupation with the forms of registration and recording cannot be emphasized enough (V, 417, 421; VI, 60-72; Stark, III, 165-166; IX, 232-264). He set out a variety of methods and types of inquiries to obtain evidence and information, including methods of collecting samples. Information, Bentham thought, must be solicited, created. Virtually every piece of his writing affords some evidence of his concern for the extensive, intricate, and scientific nature of the business (VI, 72). Bentham also attended to the way information should be passed within and among departments and legislative committees, and for this reason, he was interested in the relation between permanent and elected officials (IX, 625). Nor did he ignore the relation between local and central government on this matter (IX, 640).

21. Gilbert Highet, *The Classical Tradition* (Oxford: Oxford University Press, 1949), pp. 324-327.

22. Brougham, *Historical Sketches,* I, vii.

Index

Absolutism, 2, 5, 71, 74, 77, 78, 99-100; and popular sovereignty, 74, 80, 82, 152
Aestheticism, 8, 44, 45, 58-59, 63-71
Anarchical Fallacies, 62
Aristocracy: and classicism, 9, 59, 67; and the people, 37, 47, 79, 84, 120-130, 133, 135-136; aesthetic ideology of, 59, 65-68, 70; principle of honor, 127-132, 135, 137-139, 143. *See also* Officialdom
Aristotle, 8, 22
Asceticism, 8, 43-44, 45, 58-63, 65, 69, 70-71
Beccaria, Cesare, Marchese de, 34, 48
Benevolence, 14, 49, 65, 103, 160n33; and public service, 120-121
Blackstone, William, 9, 30, 66-67, 69-70, 76, 91
Bodin, Jean, 75-76
The Book of Fallacies, 37, 56
Brougham, Henry, 25, 119, 129, 149
Burke, Edmund, 119, 128-138, 142-143, 148-149
Burr, Aaron, 18
Classical thought, 8, 9-11, 12, 17, 21, 26; and aristocratic aestheticism, 59, 66-68. *See also* Legislator
Codes, 10, 12, 14, 18, 24, 25, 124; and legislative form, 11, 13, 19, 22-24, 95. *See also* Legislator
Command theory of law, *see* Law
Common Law, 9, 10, 18, 23, 24; criticized, 68-69, 90, 93-97, 122-126
Constitutional Code, 7, 20, 37, 53, 78-79, 80, 84, 86-87, 118, 139, 140, 141, 147, 148
Custom, 9, 43, 68-70, 92
Defense of Usury, 51
Democracy, 146-147; Bentham's preference for, 7-8, 70, 78, 84-86, 117, 151-152; distinct from popular sovereignty, 78-79, 83, 86, 87-88; popular control of governors, 83, 85-87, 133, 145-147, 163n13; and war, 108, 115
Efficiency, 35, 51, 71, 83, 110, 139; a consequence of utility, 58, 104, 106, 116, 153
Enlightenment, 3-6, 28-29, 39, 109, 110; cosmopolitanism, 1, 4, 100-101, 106, 112, 164n9
Equality: in radical psychology, 28, 29, 33, 38-39; and security, 41-42, 47-48, 50-53; of subsistence, 48-50, 52-53; and revolution, 51-52, 60-63; of states 113-116
Fanaticism: utility opposes, 24-25, 42-44, 56, 117, 152; and revolution, 43, 51-52, 60, 63, 70
Fénélon, François, 14-15, 21
Fictions, 68-70
A Fragment on Government, 30, 66, 70, 76, 86
French Revolution, 8, 57, 161n6, 162n10; and Declaration of Rights, 62-63
Government, 69, 72-73, 86-87, 98, 113, 117, 118, 151, 153, resistance to, 40-41, 79-80, 90, 91, 92; and administration, 49, 86, 118-119, 144-145; a habit of obedience, 73, 78, 92. *See also* Aristocracy; Democracy; Legislation; Public service
Halévy, Elie, 3, 7
Hartley, David, 32-33, 39
Helvetius, Claude Adrien, 29-32, 36-39, 40, 56
Hobbes, Thomas, 10, 39, 40, 47, 82, 109; on security, 40-42, 44
Honesty, 18, 21, 40-41, 58, 145; lawyers impede, 124, 127

Index

Hume, David, 10, 34, 141

International law, 105, 106, 107-108

International relations, 6, 99-117, 153; colonies, 106-107, 111, 114; balance of power, 112-114; and trade, 114-115; and public opinion, 115-116. *See also* International law; Reason of state; Utility; War

An Introduction to the Principles of Morals and Legislation, 7, 10, 12, 27-28, 31, 34, 35, 36, 38, 58, 62

Judiciary, 23, 86, 91, 134; domestic tribunal, 15-16, 96-97; function, 92-97; and legal profession, 124-126

Law, 7; higher law, 56-57, 90-91, 161n4; command theory of, 74-75, 83, 88-97; and punishment, 89-91, 141-142. *See also* Codes; Common Law; Legislation; Logic of the will

Legal Profession, 9, 30, 47, 56, 100, 124-127; and command theory of law, 75, 93-97; and lawmaking, 97-98, 119-120, 122-124, 127, 147

Legislation: ordinary, 9-10, 142; vs. education, 10, 14-15, 17-18, 20, 21, 39, 46, 52, 91; vs. ancient law, 14, 15, 17, 21, 27; secures expectations, 16, 18, 21, 24, 27, 29, 37, 41-50, 52-54, 152; specific and timely character, 16, 56, 62, 87, 118, 144-145; changeable, 17, 53, 82, 95-96, 118, 144-146, 150; and administration, 18, 118, 144-145, 148; and judiciary, 93-97

Legislator, 10, 11-12, 13-18, 19, 20, 23-24, 79, 158n8, 11; Bentham's version of, 21-25

Letters of Anti-Machiavel, 6, 26, 109-110, 113

Lind, John, 25

Locke, John, 30, 141; on psychology, 28-32, 36-37, 41, 44-46, 158n16; on property, 45, 48

Logic of the will, 22-23, 24, 88, 94, 95

Mill, John, 8

Monarchy: Bentham's view of, 7, 8, 67, 78, 134-136; and sovereignty, 75-79, 82, 83, 99; and international relations, 99, 101

Montesquieu, Charles Louis de Secondat, 19

Motives, 28, 33-36; and punishment, 27, 29, 34-36, 38, 91; and egoism, 34, 37, 39, 40; Bentham attacks, 26, 37, 56

Natural Rights, 56-57, 59, 62-63, 161n2

Of Laws in General, 91, 93

Offenses, 35, 38, 39, 40, 64-65, 94

Official Aptitude Maximized, Expense Minimized, 119, 128-129, 132, 139, 148

Officialdom, 86, 118; rewards for, 5, 6, 20-22, 23, 128-131, 137-139, 141-144, 149, 165n13; aristocratic officialdom, 119-120, 127-139, 140, 141, 142, 143, 150; services, 119-123, 139-142, 144-146; favoritism, 133-136, 138. *See also* Responsibility

Owen, Roberts, 64

Panopticon, 19-20, 39, 97

Parliament, 20, 91, 97; aristocratic, 20, 125, 134-136, 140

Plan of Parliamentary Reform, 84-85

Plato, 17

Poverty, 47-51, 52-53, 133, 160nn32-35; subsistence, 45-46, 48-51, 53, 104

Price, Richard, 141, 142

Principles of International Law, 6, 102, 105, 109

Progress, 4, 6, 39

Property, 45-48, 51-52, 60; and aristocratic government, 132-133, 137

Public service, *see* Service

Publicity, 84-85, 87, 130, 153; and international relations, 6, 110, 112, 116

Radicalism, 7-8, 30, 84-85, 113, 126, 147; philosophic radicalism, 25

The Rationale of Reward, 139

Reason of state, 4-6, 8, 72, 117; and international relations, 100, 102, 106, 108-111, 112, 115-116

Responsibility, 21; of officials, 21, 83, 86-87, 118, 119-123, 141-150; legal, 35-36, 152

Rhetoric, 26, 44, 56, 70; and law, 16, 62; and aristocracy, 66, 148-149

Ricardo, David, 25

Romanticism, 3, 142

Rousseau, Jean Jacques, 5, 19, 25, 39, 79; on the Legislator, 15, 17; on equality, 42, 46-48, 52

Security: the end of law, 29, 36, 37, 41-45, 52, 55; of property, 45-46, 48, 51-54, 60; of states, 101, 104-106, 111, 113-115, 160n38

Service, 47, 73, 138; public service, 119-122, 127, 132, 139-141, 142-143, 145. *See also*

Officialdom; Responsibility
Shelburne, Lord, 11, 25, 26, 109
Smith, Adam, 138, 141
Sovereignty, 71, 74-77, 82, 99; popular sovereignty, 74, 75, 77, 78-80, 82-88, 102; and arbitrariness, 81-82, 83; and command theory of law, 88-92, 94. *See also* Monarchy, State
State: state theory, 1-6, 7, 8, 71, 72-73, 99-100; a legal entity, 2, 6, 7, 10, 83, 117, 118, 151; a norm of order, 3, 4, 101, 116-117, 151-153; range of activities, 41-42, 49-51, 80, 145-146, 148, 151; sovereignty of, 72-73, 88, 100, 101, 105, 108-109, 116-117; consolidated, 107, 111. *See also* Utility; International relations; Security
Statistics: and legislation, 18-19, 87, 118, 144; and state activity, 50, 148, 164n1, 165n20; vs. aestheticism, 64

Supply Without Burden, 52
A Table of the Springs of Action, 33
Toleration, 3, 65; and utility, 39, 58-59, 71, 152
Utility: and diversity and change, 3, 18, 20-21, 26, 39, 57-58, 65, 150, 152; a higher rationality, 5, 9, 27, 73, 83, 117, 118; and private morals, 7, 10, 58-59, 80, 90, 157n4; a rationale for law, 7, 9, 17, 20-21, 24, 38, 55-56, 59, 93, 123, 146, 149; anti-rhetorical, 10, 25, 44, 56, 148-149; and expectations, 24, 37, 43, 96, 123; vs. aestheticism and asceticism, 44, 58-59, 64; prediction, 44, 53; and resistance, 78-79; equal utility of states, 101-106, 108, 109, 110-112, 113-114, 115-117
Voltaire, François Marie Arouet de, 10
War, 104, 105-106, 108, 111, 113, 115, 153

This book may be kept

FOURTEEN D

A fine will be charged for each day

$ILL (10-3-80)$

9 1988

NOV 20 '95

50203

M

C

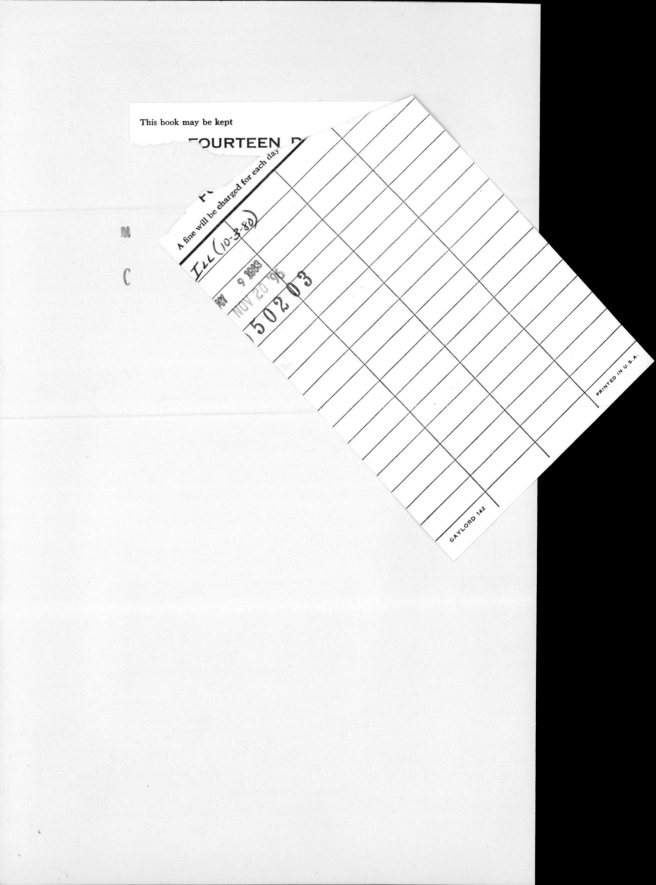

GAYLORD 142

PRINTED IN U.S.A.